Bound Like Grass

Bound Like Grass

A MEMOIR FROM THE

WESTERN HIGH PLAINS

Ruth McLaughlin

Foreword by Dee Garceau-Hagen

UNIVERSITY OF OKLAHOMA PRESS : NORMAN

The names of some people appearing in this book have been changed,
in consideration of their privacy.

Library of Congress Cataloging-in-Publication Data

McLaughlin, Ruth, 1947–
Bound like grass : a memoir from the western high plains / Ruth McLaughlin;
foreword by Dee Garceau-Hagen.
p.   cm.
Includes index.
ISBN 978-0-8061-4137-4 (hardcover : alk. paper)
1. McLaughlin, Ruth, 1947–
2. Farm life—Montana.
3. Montana—Biography.
I. Garceau-Hagen, Dee, 1955–
II. Title.
CT275.M4385A3 2010
973.3'03'092—dc22
[B]
2010004929

The paper in this book meets the guidelines for permanence and durability of the Committee on
Production Guidelines for Book Longevity of the Council on Library Resources, Inc. ∞

1 2 3 4 5 6 7 8 9 10

For Mike,
Dell, and Andy

Foreword

DEE GARCEAU-HAGEN

Ruth McLaughlin writes with a child's powers of observation, acute and unadorned. Navigating by site and memory, she explores her roots with plainspoken sensitivity, at once loving and critical. The result is a nuanced portrait of one Swedish-American family that homesteaded on the northern plains. Theirs is a twentieth-century story spanning depression, world war, and the social upheaval of the 1960s in a rural world bounded by long spaces and isolation.

McLaughlin brings a distinctive voice to the literature of homesteading that transcends geography and region. A journey of reconciliation, this memoir exposes universal human dilemmas—a father's insensitivity to his son; a mother's will to feed her family against steep odds; a brother and sister cocooned against loneliness; a daughter's ambivalence toward her own roots. With these stories, McLaughlin overturns the pioneer lore of triumph over adversity, unearthing difficult truths behind family legend about her bold immigrant grandfather.

What distinguishes this memoir from other homesteading narratives is its focus on the second and third generations, those who inherited the charge to make something of the land. McLaughlin grew up near the "high line" in Montana, where her grandfather established a claim at great cost to his family, creating a legacy of impoverishment that persisted for generations. McLaughlin's parents, the second generation, spent their lives in struggle against drought, killing winters, and the vagaries of grain markets. McLaughlin chronicles the small yet inexorable ways that poverty wore on her parents. Thrift became deprivation and deprivation crept into their emotional lives, crimping what they gave to their children. Thrift meant giving up on the eldest daughter, intelligent yet emotionally compromised. Thrift meant no support for this daughter when she left home, and no visits when she wound up consigned to an asylum in Minnesota. Poverty translated to ignorance and shame about the youngest daughter, a child with Down syndrome. Thrift gave no quarter to a son's ambitions to leave the farm. For McLaughlin, seasons turned on the cruelty of schoolmates toward her vulnerable sisters, on the exit of her angry brother, on the failing of her mother's health.

One by one, family members left the homestead, and, gradually, the impress of human will on the landscape faded. This is a story of people trying to reshape the land, and instead, the land reshaped them. It is an unusual narrative in which the humans lost and the land won. And yet there is no satisfying denouement, leaving swaths of renewed prairie behind. Native grasses reclaim the homestead, but even as McLaughlin's family exits, developers enter, and we know they will alter the landscape again, this time for corporate profit.

Still, McLaughlin reaches deeper than impoverishment and loss. She writes to the slow cadence of childhood on a farm, evoking sensual memories—sky like a "blue bowl," fence posts worn smooth where a milk cow rubbed her neck, her mother's "victory cake" dense with raisins. What, for McLaughlin, are childhood memories were for her parents a life's work. She makes palpable her parents' devotion to the land, interwoven with their marriage, and inextricable from their commitment to each other. Like the native prairie grasses that become McLaughlin's guiding metaphor, their roots grew thick and tangled beneath the soil with a strength that held fast against damaging winds, but hindered other kinds of growth. At times baffled and angered by her parents' dogged fidelity to the farm, McLaughlin also finds compassion for them, "a generation trapped between adventurous parents and discontented children." Their job, writes McLaughlin, "was to hold onto the idea that hail-battered, drought-struck small farms could support a family. They awaited the next big experiment on the northern plains: the advent of large-scale farming. My generation left to prepare the way."

Honest about hardships and failure, McLaughlin steers clear of pity. Rather, she is simply unsentimental. When an aunt from California waxes enthusiastic about the Montana farm being just like *Little House on the Prairie*, McLaughlin and her mother know better. And if the author subjects her family to scrutiny, she also turns the same unflinching gaze on herself. In mapping her disabled sisters' social and emotional isolation, McLaughlin must reckon with her own cruelty and failings toward them. This is difficult moral terrain, and makes a far more compelling story than the more conventional drama of blizzards, locusts, or prairie fire normally associated with homesteading literature. In its insight and compassion for people bent by place and their own choices, her work is akin to Ivan Doig's *This House of Sky*.

Bound Like Grass

Destiny

2001

I heard about the fire in winter, and three months later I travel the narrow highway east across the state. No traffic, only miles and miles of prairie hills, roughening at river breaks, and in long valleys stubble fields of last year's wheat. Through town after tiny town I slow, the highway tamed to a street, at last entering Culbertson just before Montana's seamless shift to North Dakota.

I continue east in slow motion toward the farm. This ten miles I've more than memorized; I feel my body tugged toward each landmark: the homestead shack, still sturdy, whose turn-of-the-century occupant, Chicago transplant Paul Bisceglia, hanged himself. In the next field is a lone tree, huge now, that someone once had swerved around with a plow. Far from water, the tree has somehow survived. I feel the pull of worn fence posts, gray as bone, some misshapen. When I was small I imagined the ugly ones as fierce, staring at me. Now as I pass they seem subdued, merely old.

Beyond them, I think I see the first gleam of spring in prairie grass. I picture our small white house on its hill, long windows overlooking our land east and west, and south half a mile to the highway. Today is sunny with just an edge of winter in chill air. The sky overhead is blank, an innocent blue, so different from that day in January when my ninety-something friend in town heard on the sheriff's scanner: "The Alexander house burning up in snow."

Then I round the last curve and see on our hill just a blackened chimney in open air. I'm shocked at how complete the fire has been.

I turn north up the gravel road whose weeds scour my car's underside. Beyond the ruins of the house, a coal shed, two garages, and the upright granary remain. On other visits here I've looked for their decline. I've half-wished for the buildings to lean and collapse, show

how to unfasten from this land. I've wanted to find a roof torn off by wind, linoleum curling up in corners of the house. Instead, the sturdy out-buildings have perpetuated the farm in my family's absence. In five years I've watched a single slow decay: down the gentle slope of hill past the long red barn, corral poles are loosening and shrugging down.

Our family had a ninety-seven-year fling here; now we are gone. Ten have been left behind, including six children, planted in two cemeteries.

I didn't think I'd feel so cheated while staring at the rubble of our house. But our farm was more than just a home. Our fenced pastures and oblong fields on slopes of hills seemed permanent, the end stage of this land: our family's destiny.

My maternal grandfather, the first of us in our corner of the state, told the story of his journey here as if it were ordained. My brother and I listened as we hoed his windbreak. Twice a year in summer, starting when we were small, Grandpa Hawkins drove Dwight and me from our neighboring farm to labor. We chopped at weeds that the disk couldn't reach, fireweed and Russian thistle smothering seedlings of blue spruce. It took five years of hoeing before the new trees that didn't belong here—vulnerable to wind and drought—outgrew the weeds that did. My grandfather refused to plant an ordinary wind-break, scrub Chinese elm and caragana, that didn't need a hoe.

Midmorning, he strode down the path to visit, overalls drooping on his small frame; he looked pleased with our chore. He recited how he'd stepped onto a ship in Sweden at age sixteen, arriving starved six weeks later in New York. He bought the first food he could find on crowded streets, fresh gingersnaps from a nickel vendor, and ate the entire bag at once, becoming violently ill. But he recovered, and found his way to Minnesota. In 1904 he boarded a train for North Dakota.

I liked the story's final chapter: how he got off the train and on again in Williston—too civilized—and at last found land across the Montana line that resembled his Swedish home, except that a dry coulee, instead of a creek, wound through it.

I heard my grandfather's unvarying tale of his long voyage here as a mantra: a recital of our family's destiny.

At the end of his story, Grandpa laughed, throwing back his head, blue eyes and gold tooth flashing, as if he'd delivered a giant joke. The laughter puzzled me. But now, stepping out of my car and crossing the prairie yard to teeter on the edge of our once-house, his laughter doesn't seem so strange.

Surely this farm, east of my grandfather's, *was* our family's destiny. Following failed homesteaders, my father was the first to make a living on the place.

Our farm's dirt roads are his, as well as the two coulees dammed for stock water, fringed by cottonwood, ash, and Russian olive. He stamped out fields north and west of our caragana and Chinese elm windbreak, alternating wheat and summer fallow, and fenced an apron of prairie pasture south to the highway and east and west to hills at the horizon.

My brother and I fled our destinies here in our teens. I wonder what I crave on all my visits. I used to enter the empty house and stroll through the kitchen with its silent cupboards, through the mint-green living room and into my little bedroom from whose wardrobe dolls gaped. In the closet of another bedroom, ghosts of my mother still hung: housedresses abandoned in the '70s when she at last joined the fashion switch to slacks.

This time an irregular small field is outlined by the foundation's concrete scar, and I revisit the rooms in memory. A till of shattered asbestos shingle overlays the burned house, like new soil. So far, nothing grows here in spring. Prairie grass has declined entrance; there's no caragana or Chinese elm, and of course no blue spruce. But I think that somewhere fireweed and Russian thistle have begun to imagine the blank soil beneath our burned house.

I identify something at my feet: glass from the kitchen light fixture, spun into a fantastic shape. I study the borders of the burn again, trying to reconstruct trash into a house, with air walls. At the far corner is my brother's room, through which a twisted metal bedstead heaves. In the living room beside the anchoring chimney is a skeletal couch. I peer beneath twists of drainpipe and stovepipe—except for shingle siding, only metal is in pieces bigger than my hand—and see the old Underwood, my mother's typewriter. It looks intact—with carriage, space bar, keys—as if equally blackened hands could settle here to write a letter, though the desk beneath has vanished.

For thirty years my mother typed weekly letters to me on the Underwood, and then on a tiny portable. The one-page letters commenced with weather: "It is so terribly dry here. Traeger's cattle keep breaking in as are starving." In a good year: "Grass so tall it waves in the pasture!"

I feel as starved as Traeger's cattle to understand my family's lives here. Why didn't my four homesteading grandparents flee following drought, deaths, and a broken marriage? What made my parents decide to stay, turning a blind eye to the region's recurrent extreme weather?

I see that just a few feet from our house there's no trash mess; the walls folded inward as they burned. I feel a tincture of childhood shame. The cramped house always seemed a reflection of my family, how we would shrink in on ourselves on trips to town, anticipating stares.

Our house was six small rooms with curtained doorways. My brother had to enter his bedroom through that of our parents. When my sister launched one of her mysterious rages, it penetrated to my top bunk, where I lay wishing that I lived in any other family and any other house.

Now I wish that the death of our house and family had followed a more dramatic course. If the house had blown up, scattering pieces in the windbreak trees and on the prairie, then years from now someone roaming this land might stumble on our durable remains. He would kick at the shield of oven door or finger the glinting saucer of the chimney's flue stop, and picture us here.

Beside me to the east and west, and south to the abrupt edge of highway, our hills seem the same: wind-dimpled, excited for spring. I'm half-surprised the prairie grass could manage a new season without our anchoring house.

Growing up, I thought these hills favored us. South across the Missouri River, my father's father nearly starved on land whose scanty soil discouraged grass and wheat.

Of course, a glacier had favored us. The last late Wisconsin glacier creeping from the north had halted just before the Missouri River:

a thousand-foot-high shelf of ice. Then—as if fashioning a template for future immigrants—it departed. Boulders fell through rotting ice, fouling our fields, just as ten thousand years later, failing homesteaders left behind a litter of shacks and machinery. But the glacier in its long retreat released a gift of Canadian silt and clay and mineral-rich rock dust, gentling the debris into long hills to grow protein-rich prairie grass and wheat.

The glacier formed our hills, grass grew; three generations of our family spent a minute of history here, then vanished.

On my last visit I stopped at Grandpa Hawkins's farm three miles west, home to the blue spruce windbreak. My grandfather's log barn and chicken coop remain; pole fences are intact. But the new owner did not bother to keep chickens or milk a cow. He erected a cavernous steel machinery shed south of the house, dwarfing it, and making insignificant my grandfather's low sheds and barn.

The owner's wife greeted me at the door. She said mysterious things had begun to appear, as if dropped from the sky or heaved from the earth like the glacial rocks we picked and dumped at corners of the fields each spring. She'd discovered a turn-of-the-century Swedish dictionary in the attic, and a *W* branding iron that I'm certain was not my grandfather's, though no one else occupied his land.

There's no one left to ask.

Now my family's farm has a new owner. He lives miles away, our land only a patch on a quilt of farms he operates with giant machines. I glimpse one beyond the granary, a hulking yellow grain drill three times the size of our John Deere model nearby. Also dwarfed beside it are my father's sickle mower and the sharp-tined dump rake. The owner's machine, seldom used here, is like scat to mark the land as his own.

Our grain drill and slender mower will join the ranks of the dead past. All around the prairie on the tops of hills, along flanks of hills and overgrown in coulees, are rusted binders, plows, and harrows left behind by fleeing homesteaders. In my childhood the tools were only a curiosity, something to fix the eye on during snail's-pace trips to town: surely the machinery's owners had not thought their destinies were here.

Our farm's new owner without notice struck the match that burned our house. For five years he had ignored my sneaking up here, ignored the museum we'd left behind. High in a cupboard was the green plastic doughnut maker my mother used just once, forming doughnuts grease-laden and small. In my dim bedroom's wardrobe were bride and groom dolls in moldering dress, a wooden black baby with a sock shirt, and Dennis the Menace. On my last visit Dennis looked jaunty still despite the absence of an arm below the elbow.

At the far end of the burned rubble I spy the dull gleam of metal ingots—knobs from my mother's 1940s waterfall veneer dresser? I zero in on the location of the snowy-channeled black-and-white TV: gone. But alongside the tipped shell of the refrigerator is a nest of broken and grayed ceramic. I think of the vaporized TV and try to imagine what could have survived the fire: electric insulators? my mother's cracked ovenware, old as her marriage?

The fire must have been immense. The skinny cottonwood behind the house, a volunteer plant with roots dug deep into the open drain field, is blistered and limbless on the fire side.

I suddenly wish that I had been here, hungry as I am for a transforming event. That's how I pictured my parents' deaths and how the end of our farm would be: suffused with meaning, an alchemy. Like fire.

Not ordinary. Not as my father, alone in his little house in town, predicted last year, saying suddenly over the phone: "I'm just afraid when you call someday I won't be here."

I look toward our windbreak. The slender trees are dying, a few tangled together as if clinging to each other in death. I'm surprised. I had thought that the trees, small-leaved in anticipation of drying winter winds, summer drought, and moisture-robbing weeds, would last forever.

Then I hear my grandfather's laughter again. It hadn't mattered that he planted an impractical blue spruce windbreak, one that switched to dying the moment he left the farm: his replacement hadn't time—or grandchildren—to hoe, haul water in a tank from town, and shovel dikes to direct spring snowmelt. Now the rows of evergreen are gap-toothed, at least every other tree dead. But a handful of them tower raggedly, visible miles away.

I look down our footpath over which pigweed has flung bright ten-tacles, beyond the little white gate to the prairie rising and falling to its seam of highway. The highway is the same, cars appearing from a long way off, passing slowly with the elegance of animals. On summer nights my parents sat outside on kitchen chairs, counting cars east and west.

Beside me in the grass, or in the burned-out skull of our house, I hear a cricket's trill. We're all gone except for me and my brother, who ended up in California. He rarely visits.

I feel like a sole survivor, a twin to the ugly cottonwood, black-blis-tered. For years we ignored the tree, my father unwilling to nurture more than a front yard spruce. We waited for the tree to die. But it lived, and thrived on our gray bath water and dishwater from the kitchen sink.

At my feet is the grave of the dirt-walled cellar, a small room en-tered separately from outside, home to potatoes over winter. Pitched into it is the kitchen coal stove, white enamel skirts blackened. I take momentary satisfaction in the huge sound its crashing down must have made, stirring our farm to life again.

In summers Dwight and I were made faint by the odors of the stove's noonday meal—frankfurters cauterized in an oven dish, pota-toes steaming. In winters we perched beside it when the road outside had vanished, a sweep of snow rising up to the barbed wire fence. We knew that the school bus would pass us by for at least a day. Back and forth our father tramped, carrying coal, his overshoes leaving a pud-dly mess on the floor. Dwight and I scooped melting snow from the linoleum and tossed it onto the stove to hiss, seeing whose pile could stay alive the longest.

Now I wonder why the new owner burned the house. The remains are dangerous if he decides to run cattle, which could topple into the open cellar. Did he want to put to rest all our ghosts? Was he tired of finding the tracks of my twice-a-year visits?

My old friend Edna said in town: "The fellow probably burned the place to keep bums out."

But I think we're all still here, wandering in and out of sheds and the grease-fouled truck garage, inhaling the granary's clean wheat scent. From the fenced pen in the pasture that once held weaner pigs, bristle-haired, squealing at our approach, I think I hear their voices carried on the wind. My hands still feel the slickness of the long manger pole inside the barn, burnished smooth by the milk cow's throat as she plunged her head over it into hay.

I turn to leave the farm again; once more I've managed to sneak onto this land with the owner absent. Then I see something in the rubble I can't place.

It's a slender bottle, old, perhaps a Hawkins souvenir saved by Mother. The bottle is sturdy, and survived better than I the conflagration of the house. "Duraglass" is embossed on one flat side.

I tip the soot-blackened bottle into my hand and glittery particles tumble out. A patent medicine hoarded by my grandparents? Another brand of the hope that brought them here?

Grandpa Hawkins's hope overrode the practicality of busting virgin sod to plant wheat. The prairie grass resisted breaking, fraying the strength of four harnessed horses. Grandpa chopped the ground with an axe to let the steel plowshare dig in, then it turned sod over in curls unbroken for a quarter-mile. He sometimes had to file a new edge on the share each night.

Borne on by glittery hope, the homesteaders did not stop to ponder the grass's resistance, its adaptation to drought and shredding hailstorms that wheat, oats, flax, and barley could not survive: long roots of native grass were bound to one another, intertwining.

Settlers in our county turned over 800,000 acres of virgin prairie— more than half the land. The work was done long before my fifties childhood, but one year when I was small the owner of a high pasture north of ours broke the sod and planted wheat. My father called the man "Eddie Sodbuster." For years, Dad spoke admiringly of how Eddie had busted sod, recalling it even after the man gave up farming and sold out. I never learned Eddie's real name.

Now Eddie Sodbuster's field, along with others, is returning to native grass, paid for by a federal conservation program. Back-to-nature could take fifty years, though the program accelerates the process by requiring landowners to knock down weeds. Thistle grows first in bare ground, choked out by sturdier pigweed and fireweed, finally overtaken by short-lived grasses that ready soil for the return of sod-forming western wheatgrass, needle-and-thread, green needle grass, and blue grama.

This century's settlers on empty Montana land are not short, wiry Scandinavians, but short, wiry prairie grasses.

In retrospect, my grandparents seem foolish, believing that tall wheat with short roots, not entwined, could buffet drought and hail and grasshoppers like native species. Some hope-in-a-bottle—such as I hold in my hand—put them under a spell.

But I am not free of the spell. I know that I will take the little Duraglass bottle home and place it in a window where I can glance at it often. I am also bound like grass here.

I'm not alone. My brother could not wait to get out, but he has kept current on farming. He knows about tractors replacing those of our era, with radios and air-conditioned cabs, and—he recently told me—global positioning systems that keep the machines from swerving more than a few inches off a straight furrow. He says that all plows are obsolete now; with "minimum tillage" the ground is barely scratched for sowing, and, instead of machinery, chemicals control weeds.

I tease Dwight about his interest. Each February he drives from Escondido two hundred miles north—bypassing Disneyland—to the World Ag Expo in California's agriculture-rich Central Valley.

"Why?" I asked this year.

"It's what I know."

Dwight and I agree we don't know much else: isolated on the farm, we did not learn to swim or dance or bowl. At his boss's Super Bowl party a few years ago, Dwight was invited by the man and his sons to step outside and toss a ball. Dwight mumbled an excuse, and could not admit he had never thrown a football or even held one.

Do I return to this empty farm because it is what I know?

I drive long miles here, leaving normal family life behind in Great Falls. Or what I hope is normal: school sports and clubs, and music lessons are all new to me, and I sweat the details. "Is this how you do birthday parties?" I asked my daughter as we arranged her first one. She was a veteran of several at six years old.

I think of Grandma Hawkins, who perhaps suffered the most here but still seemed bound to her land. Short and plump, her legs encased year-round in cotton stockings, she snugged a man's billed cap over her iron-gray bun and roamed the farm between chores.

Long ago, she had waited impatiently in Minneapolis to join Kyrle Hakkansson, a fellow Swede, on his Montana land. "How I envy you being out doors all the time breathing pure air," she wrote from her housemaid's attic room. She addressed her letters to "Charles Hawkins," the new name Kyrle had chosen before heading west. She penned, "We can dance in that lovely air."

I liked to accompany my grandmother on her walks around the farm, skipping ahead, then slowing to her arthritic pace. In spring we searched for crocus in the pasture, heading north through the corral past the windmill with its weeping wooden tank in which she drowned kittens each year. I avoided the tank when alone, believing it was depthless. Meadowlarks, returned in spring, teetered near on fence posts. Grandma interpreted for me their liquid song: "Oh, you're a pretty-little-girl."

We looked for low-growing purple crocus, so beautiful and brief it seemed not to belong here; the plant was soon succeeded by homely sunflower, milkweed, and wild onion. Its plump blossoms were the only ones Grandma picked, lasting a few days in a small dish. Friends have encouraged me to plant crocus in my backyard. But I've never believed a nursery plant would be the same as the solitary one that broke through brown prairie after numbing winter, sometimes pushing up in snow.

Grandma would halt at a spot in the pasture where the windbreak dwindled to three currant bushes; I knew to imitate her silence there. Every summer blossoms, then berries, appeared on the bushes. I'd seen the ruby glow of currant jelly on a neighbor's cellar shelf, but my grandmother never robbed these trees for jelly.

Crocus erupted, meadowlarks sang, hills all around heaved and fell in memory of another time, as we paused at three babies' graves.

Childhood Years

Hunger

Noon and night we ate what my glass-half-empty brother called peasant food: mashed potatoes, canned vegetables, and processed meat. For snacks we were allowed saltine and graham crackers and a cookie with two chocolate chips inside baked by our frugal mother. If she had splurged in town, we drew three M&Ms from a ten-cent package on the refrigerator shelf. The red M&Ms went first, followed by brown.

Despite the unvarying menu, I arrived at our round table with an exquisite hunger: the last meal had been served five hours before. We waited as our mother ferried steaming dishes; then we hunched over faded Melmac plates on which no smear or scrap of food would remain. No one said he liked or hated anything; no one was admonished to eat less or more. My father in overalls ate swiftly, fueling himself for the fields; in winter he readied himself to fork hay and break stock-tank ice. I bumped my sister's elbow on the cracked oilcloth; my father on my left bumped mine. We weren't a family of touchers, no hugs, kisses, tucks goodnight, though when my father was struck by a humorous story—something plucked from his blighted childhood— he might rest a plate-sized hand on my mother's shoulder; occasionally it landed like a soft claw on mine.

Something mean in our family was suspended when we squeezed

around the table for a meal. My sister, Rosemary, and I sat against the wall, flanked by the deep freeze and dusty mirrored buffet. I averted my eyes from the slop pail wedged beneath the washstand shelf, and alongside it the puddle rags—damp, reptilian—waiting to smear away mud or manure tracked in the door. I could ignore the oilcloth abrading my bare arms, and my family's sweat smell. My mother's cooking was even a drug for prickly Rosemary, silent at meals. Only Dwight at times broke the trance, inquiring why we couldn't have tuna noodle casserole, sloppy joes, or spaghetti like school friends. My mother lifted her eyes to stare at him across the table. She didn't disagree, but I knew more variety wouldn't happen.

Below us, beneath the scuffed linoleum of the kitchen floor, a thousand pounds of potatoes lay in dirt. My father planted fifty pounds of seed potatoes in spring, then we invariably ate the harvest all year long as if we were part of the potato life cycle. Our two dogs shared leftovers, and the chickens—which, like my brother, seemed always restless, hungry—ate the peels. The potatoes lasted well through winter in the cellar's dank air. In summer they began to sprout, but my mother rehabilitated their soft and wizened bodies into family meals.

We were allowed a single frankfurter—the fat red ones were my favorite, burst open from the coal stove's heat—or one baloney slice. I loaded up on mashed potatoes. Finally, our mother rose to carry in dessert, crowning all our plain meals and created from half of her three-by-five recipe cards, velvety from overuse, stored in a tin box. Dishes of chocolate, butterscotch, or tapioca pudding had a cookie or square of cake tipped into each. On Monday, wash day, when she hadn't time to cook, rice, milk, raisins, and eggs baked themselves to pudding in the oven. We had blonde and chocolate brownies, yellow and chocolate cakes. Sunday we had Jell-O with fruit cocktail; Dwight and I tried to identify the fruit in dice-like squares. We had servings of our farm's own fruit almost each day: rhubarb sauce, pie, crisp, or crunch.

In the middle of winter when the chickens refused to lay eggs, huddling instead on their roosts, some falling dead from cold, we ate eggless, sugarless victory cake from a faded wartime recipe. The honey-sweetened loaf was chewy with raisins and dense; I felt myself in a dark time my mother still spoke of wonderingly: of Roosevelt on the radio, ration books, a time when the tall neighbor boy, a cut-up in school, vanished forever on the fields of distant France.

Winter was our season of abundant milk, the milk cow freshening. My mother tried new recipes clipped from *Ladies Home Journal* and *Dakota Farmer*, our two magazines. She made blancmange, pronouncing it "blank mainge." I was sure that the pale, bland pudding's name derived from its resemblance to shining bald spots of disease on cats and cows.

When the milk cow gave birth on clean straw in the barn, we said good-bye to months of powdered milk, and welcomed whipped cream on our desserts. We also said hello to chocolate mousse. "Chocolate mouse," Mother called it; the color recalled mice darting in darkness when we entered sheds and the barn.

We had to be patient for new milk. The milk cow's calf had to suck the first antibody-rich colostrum, without which he would not survive. Then he was penned out of sight from his mother at the far end of the barn, and when the weather warmed he was staked inside our yard. It was my job in summer to mix up a powdered replacement in the nipple bucket, then brace myself as the calf rushed toward it, almost strangling himself at the chain's end. The calf gave little butts as he sucked, as I'd seen calves in the pasture do toward their mothers. All day long he would lunge toward me, even at my empty-handed approach, rubbing his face on my jeans as I scratched his head. Beneath the collar his neck was hairless, not from mange but from straining forward on his chain. In the pasture calves idly nosed into soft udders, and stood patiently as mothers tongued along their backs, swirling hair into "cowlicks." After rubbing the staked calf's head a few minutes, I would grow impatient and pull away. It did not occur to me that we had stolen more from the calf than our breakfast milk and cream for French desserts.

Once a year we drank bitter milk. Biscuitroot appeared early in spring, its sunny yellow flowers waving high above dull grass. The milk cow preferred it. Then the prairie dried, the weeds shrank, and ordinary grass prevailed. But for weeks we drank bad milk. It fouled our cereal; I even thought I could taste it in the cold pancakes we kids ate, leftovers from our parents' dawn breakfast. Rosemary, Dwight, and I begged Mother to make milk from the Carnation box on the cupboard shelf. She poured herself a drink of milk from the refrigerator's Mason jar and swore she couldn't taste anything. Only when we refused milk at meals and ate our Cornflakes dry did she break down and mix up bland, delicious powdered milk.

In summer, fresh vegetables appeared on our table: brilliant green peas that Mother boiled with a single pod to intensify the flavor, giant beets she cooked whole—sometimes for an hour or more—then slipped from their skins onto our plates. They bled sweetly as we carved them like steak. Our cows didn't provide us with steak, sold in fall for cash instead.

At a certain time of summer, just for a week or two, we had field corn in its milky, infant stage. Dwight and I rushed to gather it as Mother heated water in the giant canner for our meal. We picked three ears apiece for our sister, mother, and father, then six or seven each for the two of us. We would eat them all and remain rail thin. We stripped the corn of husks and silk, which we dumped outside the fence on the ash pile where nothing grew. A cow browsing along the dry prairie would discover it. She wolfed down each morsel of the fresh, green shucks, then suffered diarrhea that we had to be alert for outside the yard fence.

The season was brief; corn soon hardened to its dent stage. Our father shelled the kernels and then fed them through the ancient grinder, once belonging to his father, bolted to the granary floor. In winter months our teeth crackled on our mother's gravelly cornbread.

One winter when I was seven, I was eating supper at the table, soaking up the heat from the food and from the nearby coal stove—at its zenith in late afternoon, when I suddenly thought hard about peas. I studied the cooked canned peas on my plate, pale and soft atop dinner's leftover mashed potatoes on which they had been heated. I liked canned peas, collapsing in my mouth with a salty tang, exotic as far-off California from which they had arrived. They were different from our own plump peas on summer vines. But I suddenly understood that the peas before me were the same as our own bright green peas that we kids rushed to gather, shelling them as our mother boiled water. Their intensity of taste rivaled dessert.

It wasn't just our Wednesday peas, I realized at that moment, but the commercial cubed beets we ate on Fridays were once the same as the huge beets we plucked early in the mornings in late summer, shaking off garden dirt. Our winter vegetables were the same ones we ate in summer. Around me my parents and brother and sister bent industriously over their plates, as if each was cultivating a tiny acre. The world suddenly felt small.

Once or twice a year our family ate out, always at the Farmer's Union Co-op Cafeteria in Williston across the Dakota line. We climbed the rickety stairs above the Co-op Grocery after a morning of shopping—for me crossing and recrossing Main Street to compare toys on Woolworth's and Ben Franklin's low shelves. We kids were allowed hamburgers, which Dwight and I made a meal: first we ate the buttery top bun, then each piquant pickle; finally we carved the meat and bottom bun with fork and knife.

Our real eating-out treat was with our Hawkins grandparents, where we were often invited for holidays, and in the slow season of winter for Sunday meals. We already ate there most Saturdays, just a snack following our trip to bathe in their indoor bathroom. "Bath lunch," our grandmother called it, loading cookies onto a plate to our mother's mild protests. Grandma said that we children were "depleted" by our weekly bath, making me feel weak on the couch, where I waited for the crackle of cellophane on pantry shelves.

Grandma's cookies were store-bought. She rarely baked them, because she was arthritic, or perhaps because Dwight and I could easily down a dozen each. I loved town cookies—Vienna Fingers and Dutch Windmills, and my favorite, a round wafer topped by a pink marshmallow sponge.

Dwight and I ate quickly, competing. Also on the table was a pitcher of lukewarm Kool-Aid, prepared hastily; speckles of flavor, like jewels, rested on its sandy sugar bottom. My brother and I strategically filled and refilled our glasses, trying to be the winner of the pitcher's final sweet swill.

My brother and I prepared for Sunday dinner at our grandparents' place by going light on breakfast pancakes, surprising our mother but delighting the recipients of leftovers, Bullet and Nip, who gulped pancakes down whole. Just before noon we stepped outside into frigid air and crossed the rutted yard with its remains of snow. We squeezed into our car—always an out-of-style used one that advertised our family's modest means. We owned a slope-backed '49 Chevrolet in 1953 when boxlike cars were popular; when we could afford a '53, new models were long and sleek.

Dad drove in slow motion, turning west onto the narrow highway and following its quiet length three miles until he turned up the alley of windbreak trees and parked at its end. We spilled from the car and seated ourselves at our grandparents' table, round like our own. I was ravenous.

My grandmother trudged in, carrying dishes from the narrow counter and coal stove: mashed potatoes, sweet potatoes, packaged sweet rolls, Jell-O salad, two freshly killed and roasted chickens; also gravy, which my mother, who did not like it, seldom made.

In the cramped kitchen, yellow like ours with pink instead of green linoleum below, we bowed our heads in a kind of worship over crowded plates, and began.

Food was serious, we knew. Dad could access memories of near-starvation in the drought of the 'teens on his father's marginal homestead—a location chosen by Grandfather Alexander for its sweeping views. In the 1918–19 winter the family subsisted on "graveyard stew"—made from vegetables softening in the cellar. My nine-year-old father fainted from hunger at school, "a kind of spasm," Grandfather noted in his diary. From the poor diet, Dad developed sores on his arms that would not heal. Grandfather detailed that year's Thanksgiving menu: jackrabbit hash, string beans, bread dipped in Karo syrup, cucumber pickles, carrot pie, and tea. He later wrote: "We quit eating jacks when I found they had tapeworms."

Grandfather Alexander's failed venture was a presence even at Grandma Hawkins's crowded table. From her perch on a stool at the cluttered counter, she entreated us to eat more. She rose to offer the last of the sweet potatoes to my father but he waved her off, stirring his coffee and gazing past us out the window, his prelude to falling into silent brooding or erupting with a funny tale.

Dwight and I ate steadily. Even in our parents' penurious household, good eating was aligned with health and strength. On my third and final helping I spread mashed potatoes to the plate's rim, and troweled on thick milk gravy.

My mother and grandmother rose to wash dishes, talking calmly, mysteriously able to dip hands into the sizzling water in pans on the hot stove. At last everyone retreated to the living room. Grandma settled into her wooden rocker; she and my mother continued a desultory conversation. My father and grandfather sat opposite on a chair and couch, Grandpa occasionally managing to penetrate Dad's thoughts and start a conversation. Rosemary, usually calm after meals, paged through old magazines.

Dwight and I bundled up and stepped outside. Sun glittered on snow. We went to view tracks in the windbreak—deer, rabbit, mice, sometimes a porcupine whose tail swept the snow like a broom. We peeked into sheds and barns. We looked at machinery identical to our own, but because it was not our own it had a kind of freshness.

Our machinery, in sheds and in a row inside the windbreak, I thought of as brooding, benign animals, but Dwight saw something more. He seemed to look into the coursing heart of machines; his breath slowed. Machinery was part of something wrong between Dad and Dwight. Even when Dwight was small he would not concede our father's quick anger toward farm implements, how Dad fell to cursing a crippled engine as if it were a dumb beast refusing to obey.

We opened the low chicken-house door to feel the warmth of compact white bodies crowded on roosts; our nostrils filled with the droppings' acrid smell. Chickens looked at us piercingly.

Indoors again, Dwight and I lay along the walls of the living room on its thin carpet, waiting for the pain in our stomachs to pass. Conversation drifted, rising out of long silence and absorbed by it again. Mother and Grandma traded weekly letters from Aunt Claire in California, a single typed page to each. They were dense with minutiae of Claire's life: meals prepared, the headaches of elementary teaching, her lucky purchase of a bushel of pears to put up in jars, the seldom-changing desert weather. Mother lowered her letter with a dreamy, absorbed look, as if she had been in the actual presence of plump, bright-lipsticked Claire.

I felt as snug as the chickens in their house. Town, where angry blowups by Rosemary drew stares, seemed distant. An edge between Dad and Dwight was absent. Our parents and grandparents mostly ignored us kids; still, I felt carried along on the current of their mysterious grownup ways. In the crowded room I inhaled our warm bodies' scent, pungent as cellar apples.

Three hours after dinner Grandma rose, and following micelike rustling in the kitchen, called us to eat again. She had spread her tropical-flowered "lunch cloth" on the table and placed dishes of Jell-O with ice cream around. Cookies waited on a plate. I wasn't hungry again, but I squeezed between my parents on a chair.

Though our grandparents provided sumptuous meals—smells of dinner still hung in the air as we hiked up our chairs for an afternoon snack—after fifty years of farming they were still poor. They had held on through the 'teens when half of new settlers left the state—disabused of the notion that rain follows the plow—and through the Dirty Thirties. Those who remained practiced "diversified farming," hedging bets between cattle and wheat. In good crop years our family lived on cash from wheat; in bad years we sold part of the herd to survive.

My grandparents never traded up their furniture or bought a nice car. My grandfather's overalls wore patches. Grandma darned socks at night with a glossy black darning egg inserted into heel or toe. But her meals did not suggest lack or want.

My parents slowly spooned up Jell-O and dripping ice cream; Dwight and I cleared the cookie plate. Then we rose and packed ourselves into the car again, and arrived at the familiarity of home. The dogs, hysterical, greeted us. Sometimes when we had been gone all day they could not express how much they missed us, could not bear to meet us as we exited the car. Our black dog Bullet hurled himself around the yard, his golden mother following, diving at imaginary sparrows—shadows of fence posts on snow.

At home I felt ill. But at bottom was the pleasure of abundance:

something in our lives had been not too little but too much. After awhile my brother and I would take turns visiting the outhouse with diarrhea. Or, like the cows who accidentally stumbled on the sweet green remains of corn, we relieved ourselves in the pasture coulee.

When I slipped into bed that night my stomach was calm. I didn't regret the feast of the day.

Our mother didn't cook big feasts; even holiday dinners had a parsimonious stamp. We usually had meatloaf, pre-carved in narrow slices, and never sweet rolls or cookies from town. Rarely gravy. My brother recalls a turkey dinner of a turkey drumstick we all shared. Later, Bullet and Nip fought over the splintery bone.

My mother's sweet tooth prompted her sole extravagance. On Sundays in winter she made fudge, and once a year at Christmas she made fudge, butterscotch, white divinity, and penuche—brown sugar fudge with cream. She fed us candy at intervals on our holiday vacation from school. Sometimes the fudge didn't harden and she served it on a spoon: Rosemary, Dwight, and I, seated on the couch, leaned like baby sparrows toward her fudge-heaped spoon. For Christmas we wouldn't receive toy guitars, Tonka trucks, or electric trains. For me a Betsy Wetsy doll never appeared. Once I got a rubber ball unconcealed in paper wrapping, and in high school Kleenex and cold cream. I remember few other Christmas gifts, but I remember Mother's candy.

In his teens Dwight declared that our parents lacked ambition; our father worked hard but not smart. He said that Mother worked harder at being cheap than she did at raising chickens or tending her garden. I knew he might be right, but I hated the criticism. Our parents kept afloat on what they had. I kept afloat on their approval. Dwight could not change that. When he left home he worked and saved smart by living in a California flophouse hotel while pouring most of what he earned into real estate.

He treated us to dinner on one visit home. Not at the Farmers Union Cafeteria or even at the new Skelly Truck Stop at Williston's edge, but at the barnlike State Line Club still straddling the prairie where Montana and North Dakota meet. The club served cocktails, prime rib, and shrimp, familiar to us from TV. The "Longest Bar in the Northwest" extended into the dining room where only a couple of people sat on a Wednesday night, making it seem longer. But even in the empty room our parents weren't at ease. Dad ordered a hamburger steak, the cheapest meal; Mother inquired of Dwight if she could have her usual bacon, lettuce, and tomato sandwich. Dwight acquiesced but told me he felt like his hard-earned money was wasted; he'd wanted our family to just once feel worthy of a good meal.

In 1966, when I first lived on my own, waitressing in Missoula following my first college year, I tried to imitate family meals. I boiled potatoes—as much for their aroma and their gurgle in the pan as for their taste. I discovered vivid green frozen peas, a facsimile of fresh.

I returned from work in late afternoon, and slipped off my white nylon dress to lie in my darkened room. I was glad to earn money in Missoula, and glad to escape the heat of outdoor work and kitchen chores. But all my days of waitressing seemed depressingly the same.

That summer I felt inside me the slow shift of chores at home: tall grass cut in June, raked into windrows, and stacked; in July, weeds disked in fallow fields, and lawnlike new wheat sprayed for grasshoppers. Finally in August harvest began, often on the sixth, Dwight's birthday.

I ate what I wanted after work and gained weight. I found a store that carried fat red franks, and downed three or four at once. I bought half gallons of ice cream that I spooned from the box, huddled in bed to keep warm; I'd never had more than two scoops at once on top of Jell-O. Trembling from cold, my lips and tongue numb, I stopped just short of finishing the carton.

I could finally have all the ice cream that I wanted, I could turn bright red from franks (my brother maintains that the nitrates from our years of processed meat will keep us pink in our coffins long past death). But neither restored my depleted self as had my grandmother's bath lunch.

Now on visits to the empty farm I struggle to see clearly. I don't want Aunt Claire's shifting memory. Her love of the 1970s *Little House on the Prairie* TV series, a feel-good upgrade of the Laura Ingalls Wilder books, gave my mother a slow burn. Claire wrote from California that the well-scrubbed characters' small failures and large triumphs reminded her of home. Mother said, "I don't remember it that way at all."

On Sundays with my grandparents I was content; I didn't hunger for anything more. Rosemary's anger would erupt again in town or school, and a mood of worry might lower over my parents as soon as we reached home. But for a time worry was absent. I felt suspended in a net of family. Like the slender roots of prairie grass, we were strengthened by being bound together.

I still like potatoes that I tug in brown plastic bags into my grocery cart. I am relieved to be away from the heat and sweat and sunburn of hoeing and knocking off potato bugs, but these store potatoes seem like orphans, far from the fields in which they grew.

Bully

In our first years, Rosemary, Dwight, and I were alone. Our grandparents to the west were three miles away. North of us was pasture, leading to Indian land; sometimes we saw distant cattle or a tractor. East of us a farm was often empty: a family with some contention preferred town. South, the highway and railroad separated us from clustered neighbors. We believed the high tracks also kept away rattlesnakes denning in rough country south along the river, making us almost snake-free.

We filled our days. Each day seemed to have exactly the hours needed to observe animals and changing weather, insects scurrying; to walk on the prairie, avoiding cactus on the slopes of hills; to inspect darkened sheds and our long, low barn.

We began school. One by one, a year apart, we boarded the yellow bus that hove into sight along our dusty road, each day startling and enraging anew our two dogs. In school I began to wonder about Rosemary. I would look up from the shouts and swirls of play to find her standing alone. Then one day at recess Terry Lorentsen, breathless in a game of tag, stopped to say: "Your sister's crazy."

Until then I had only noticed that I was stronger and faster than she, two years older. We slept together in a scarred metal bed, our legs sometimes intertwining. Because she ran slowly with an awkward gait, we didn't play together like I did with Dwight.

When Grandma Hawkins brought over suit coats rescued from the town dump, Dwight and I put them on with cowboy hats and called ourselves Texas Rangers. We mounted our bikes with cap guns in hand to race over our farm's dirt roads after ill-defined criminal strangers. We spectacularly crashed our bikes. We relished scrapes and bruises and gravel-embedded palms, proof of the seriousness of our play.

With Rosemary I cut out catalog paper dolls, perfect two-boy, two-girl families. We held tea parties at the tractor-orange play table built by our dad. We drank tap-water tea and ate graham crackers that I nibbled into fancy cookie shapes.

Her weakness made me feel safe; our play never dissolved into blows as did mine with Dwight. Her physical tentativeness reminded me of newborn calves or kittens, though she did not improve. No one else in our community resembled her; I had no one to measure her against.

We played dress-up, digging through old clothes on our mother's closet floor. I helped Rosemary into a rayon jersey church dress that I snugged into place with a safety pin as her fingers fumbled. In the narrow full-length mirror I tried to see us as grown-up sisters, Mother and Claire. Rosemary dropped her head; even then she did not like to view herself in a mirror.

She was always short, and pale even in summer. Her white blonde hair was cut Dutch boy-style by our mother. I admired her deep blue eyes. But her voice had a hoarse, unattractive timbre, and her round, blunt-featured face often wore an anxious look. Mother said once, "She was born old."

Her birth had been scheduled, labor induced, a convenience offered to women far from the hospital in Williston across the Dakota line. Labor went too fast or too slow, or a mistake was made on the turbulent day of her birth: on August 13, 1945, the United States had received Japan's peace offer; the end of World War II was near. "The nurses were just crazy," Mother recalled. She waited all day, swatting flies from her bed, for her baby whisked away at birth to be returned: "Rosemary had fever and sure worried about her," she wrote in her diary. Ten days later the baby went home; then for months Mother recorded bad news:

"Rosemary had colic all day.

"Rosemary cried all day practically.

"Rosemary had spells.

"Rosemary didn't sleep all day.

"Rosemary had colic all day. Bill told her stories."

On Rosemary's two-month birthday, Mother observed, "Rosemary won't smile or coo." She carried her concern to a Williston doctor, who x-rayed the baby's head: "Skovholt said Rosemary was okay." The next year my parents drove Rosemary 150 miles east to Minot: "Found out nothing," and two hundred miles south to a Miles City clinic: "Was physically and mentally OK they said."

The exams were brief, squeezed into a doctor's crowded schedule; Mother didn't like to pay long-distance charges for appointments. Dad added to the pressure of the visit, anxious to return home by five o'clock. Arriving late, he'd find the milk cow bawling in the corral with milk streaming from engorged teats.

The trips were my parents' last efforts to find help for Rosemary. Even when school days brought new trouble, my mother and father never had Rosemary examined again.

Shouldn't they have moved heaven and earth to find treatment for their child? Dwight and I have long chafed at our parents' passivity—cowed by events as if they deserved failed crops and damaged children.

We admired our homesteading grandparents instead, even the train wreck of Grandfather Alexander throwing over a hard-won education—eighteen years of work alternating with study to get himself through high school and the University of Minnesota—to seek land. He resigned a job as superintendent of schools in Morristown and persuaded our gentle grandmother, a former teacher in his school, to pack up two small children and start life anew in the empty West. How brave he was to strike out!

My brother and I liked to finger the stiff gray print, snapped by an itinerant photographer, of our tall grandfather shingling the roof of his new home. "The Start" was inked on the photo in his fine hand. Past the tiny house a sea of grass lies unbroken all the way to the horizon.

Dwight and I did not realize that our father's defects—his shyness, reserve, and fears—were collateral damage of our grandfather's bold move. The start of Grandfather's farm on rocky land south of the Missouri River, his venture into "scientific agriculture" that he'd read about in Minnesota, was the finish of his family. Six years after homesteading, my grandmother left to teach in rural schools, taking her daughter with her. She left behind my father to be raised by my austere grandfather, who subscribed to the *Congressional Record* and read the Bible in three languages—but did not know how to raise a son.

✳

Rosemary was mute till she was three years old, then suddenly began to speak. At age five, sitting in her rocker by the kitchen coal stove, she taught herself to read, plucking tin cans from their discard bucket behind the stove and matching words to pictures. In first grade she devoured classroom readers but seemed baffled by math, leaving worksheets blank. "Naughty," the teacher wrote in a note home, "won't do her sums."

That year a boy gliding by at recess whispered to her: "Dummy." Rosemary twirled and clumsily kicked at him, then burst into tears. The teasing began.

Boys poked her in the classroom or tugged her hair. They laughed at the formality of her speech, her expert grammar. Her own laughter was loud and turned heads. Teasing sent her into tearful rages that teachers could not quell; she was exiled to the hallway or dark cloakroom till her mood was spent.

In school I hated noon recess when the first three grades mingled. I sat with other first-grade girls on the merry-go-round; after lazily dragging our feet, a couple of us would rise to pump and renew its twirling.

Suddenly, over the din of play I would hear, "Stop! Do not touch me! Do not call me names!"

Girls craned their necks to stare. In the dirt yard surrounding our bell-towered school, children in swings, on their knees shooting marbles, or hypnotic on see-saws, stopped their play. Some joined the widening circle around Rosemary; others in stalled swings or atop the towering slide cocked their heads.

Finally, a teacher stepped in. Then the first-grade girls turned back to our circle of play, but not without looking curiously at me, as if I were a piece of the puzzle of my sister. I tried to make my face a blank.

Dwight and I did not tease Rosemary, but we took advantage of her defects. If one of us carried in cake after dinner the smallest piece would be slipped to Rosemary, who did not protest. She did not fight over cake or treats, or elbow for a window seat in the car.

One summer Grandpa Hawkins brought us three weaner pigs to raise, a new venture. We kids would sell the pigs in fall and keep the profit. We pressed against the new wire pen to watch the pigs, no bigger than puppies, race unhappily about. We tried to sort out one for each of us, but black marks were still baby-pale on white bristled hides. The next morning one pig was gone; just two pigs snuffled in resignation to their new quarters. Our father delivered the news. A pig had escaped in the night; at dawn Dad had found it a quarter-mile west, drowned in the dam. Dwight and I met each other's glance: "That one was Rosemary's."

At twelve Rosemary entered seventh grade, moving to the adjacent brick building housing junior high through high school. That same year newspaper accounts appeared of Negro students trying to integrate the high school in Little Rock, Arkansas. I read about gangs of boys that stalked the Little Rock Nine in hallways and at lunch and after school, and felt a shock of the familiar. I didn't know what it was to be a Negro, nor had I ever seen one. But I knew these boys. The boys in our school didn't slam Rosemary into lockers, throw acid in her face, or tip soup on her at lunch. But they did spit on her from a second floor landing, trip her, hide her school books, and call her names.

When I moved over to seventh grade I watched a group of junior boys, look-alikes in narrow-belted gabardine slacks and button-collar shirts, jostle Rosemary, and then when she dropped a book one of them launched it down the polished hallway with his foot. In the school basement one day Rosemary was headed toward the Home Ec. room when a laughing boy shoved his friend toward her: "He wants to ask you to the prom." From down the hall I saw the boy's mirthful look below his blonde crew cut. Rosemary, wearing a cotton dress made in Home Ec. that hung on her badly, halted. I noticed that her school shoes were broken down from her awkward gait, though the year was not half over.

Rosemary turned toward the boys. She could not learn; time and again some attention ignited hope in her face. The boys were playing a mild version of what the Little Rock Nine called "herky-jerky": a white girl would act friendly toward a new black girl, greeting her for a few days, then harshly reject her.

In the middle of the basement hallway, Rosemary smiled at the jostling boys. Suddenly, the round bell on the wall above them clanged, and they leaped through the doors of the cavernous Vo-Tech room.

From the end of the hallway I wanted to mouth my mother's plea to Rosemary at home: "Can't you just ignore them?" Only a handful of kids were friendly to her in school, mostly girl classmates. After hot lunch they primped and groomed in the basement lavatory, lifting and arranging curls before the long mirror as Rosemary watched, hoping to catch someone's eye.

The prettiest one, a cheerleader with sleek nyloned legs and a smooth shell of brown hair, sometimes smiled at Rosemary and said, "Are you ready for Mr. Nicola?"

The high school English teacher for one year, olive-skinned Mr. Nicola, was an exotic in our largely Scandinavian community. He was crush material for more girls than Rosemary—another fresh-minted teacher who would cut his teeth in our remote district and then flee. Rosemary threw back her head and laughed: "You jest!"

I never knew when I would leave a class to find hallway clamor. Someone trooping by had only to snap off a pencil lead protruding from Rosemary's binder to ignite her rage. Perhaps no more than a dozen of the fifty boys in high school participated, but their numbers seemed larger. Onlookers stopped to stare as she wept, her face bloating. She scolded in the direction of perpetrators now melted into the crowd: "It is inconsiderate to destroy property!" Then a teacher appeared, students hurried off to class, and Rosemary was sent to her study hall desk to recover.

I was sometimes bullied; boys in my class stole pencils, punched, and tripped me. I knew to ignore them and not fan the flames. I told myself the bullying was a copycat crime—boys trying out on me what their older brothers did to Rosemary.

Perhaps I fed the flames. I was tense in school, anxious for teachers' approval. I won spelldowns and shot up my hand to be first to answer questions in math class, considered a domain for boys. I wanted to show teachers I wasn't like another Alexander girl they knew.

Some teachers were impatient with Rosemary, extra trouble in school; some, like a new Home Ec. teacher, tried to help.

Mrs. Gaustad, my mother's age, a prettier version of her with short curls, had returned to teaching after a disappointing marriage. She set about making Rosemary sew a perfect dress; she wouldn't let her off the hook as other teachers had. She asked my mother to buy three yards of wool plus taffeta lining: dashing Mother's hopes for a winter project of two-yards-for-a-dollar percale.

In class Mrs. Gaustad stood at Rosemary's elbow, helping her guide fabric through the machine. She snatched up a seam ripper to slash an errant stitch or snarl of thread; Rosemary sewed seams two and three times. She came home tired from school.

Other girls in class finished their projects and moved on to pies and breads; Rosemary still labored. The sewing machine's slow-speed groaning caused the girls, pinching piecrust into pretty fluted edges, to call out that they would help. Mrs. Gaustad shook her head.

Finally, Rosemary's royal blue sheath dress was done. It sagged a little on her blunt body, though Mrs. Gaustad had tailored the pattern. She phoned Mother to ask if she would drive Rosemary to the Make It Yourself with Wool contest sponsored by sheepmen each year. "Drive to Wolf Point?" I heard Mother say doubtfully. She was a nervous driver even on the short jog to Culbertson. I got an idea. I waved and gestured, and, to my surprise, Mother agreed that I could drive Rosemary fifty miles to Wolf Point alone.

On a clear Saturday we set out, turning west on the highway toward town. Grass in ditches along the narrow road and on long hills was still brown, not yet conceding to spring. Fields were empty except for stalks of straw; the sky was blank. I felt soothed. Then I met a car and clutched the steering wheel in a death grip: my license was new, and I'd driven only once before on the highway.

Rosemary was quiet in her corner of the car. Last night I'd helped her wash her hair, then Mother trimmed her blonde bangs; the too-short bangs gave her a startled look. I'd made a row of pin curls that this morning seemed less like curls than tortured twists and turns in her hair. Still, she looked almost pretty—pale features set off by the vivid blue of her dress.

I felt happy riding with her in the car, the empty landscape wash-ing over us. Long ago, before the pressures of school, I had been fond of my sister, and I believed she was fond of me. I thought of Mother's sister Claire, who drove from California every third year to visit. Red-haired with chunky jewelry, she wasn't like Mother at all. Yet they wandered together around the farm, Claire in nice shoes, and made frivolous trips to town. Once we kids went along, scattering to walk the aisles of two grocery stores and Culbertson Drug. I finished early and rushed back to talk to Mother and Claire in the car. I felt like an intruder: they were leaned together deep in conversation, and turned only reluctantly to me.

I smiled at Rosemary and she smiled back. Then just as quickly, guilt undercut the moment's pleasure: my older sister should be driv-ing me.

Past Culbertson the highway changed, going up and down coulees of the Big Muddy drainage, dry most of the year. We came upon a slow car, someone like our dad, or Grandpa Hawkins, who drove thirty-five down the road peering into distances: "Say, is that crested wheat grass?"

I decided to stay behind the car. It wasn't going so slow, after all. Had I been speeding? I'd forgotten to watch the dial.

Then I changed my mind. I felt a great urge to bomb past the car. I hadn't yet tried to pass a car. I felt a tie to Rosemary again, young like me; we'd leave the oldsters behind. I punched the gas and shot around the car, then slipped back to the right lane. BEEP! In the rearview mirror I saw a shocked man's face close, very close. I'd turned back too soon. My foot was frozen on the gas. The man pumped his brakes—we did not hit. I looked over at Rosemary, whose eyes, dark with fear, met mine. I did not ease up on the pedal till the man's car was far behind me. Then I drove in slow motion the rest of the way to Wolf Point.

The contestants were treated to lunch in the Wolf Point school gym. Rosemary and I sat alone. Girls from small towns all around sat at tables laughing and exchanging names; they glanced at us, then looked away.

At last the style show began. At Rosemary's turn she mounted short steps to the stage, and wobbled awkwardly across in low pumps. At the end of the day she was awarded a ribbon for "Most Versatile Costume" in the senior division, passed over for "Best Constructed" and "Most Beautiful Use of Wool." She stepped onto the stage again to polite applause.

She posed with nine other winners for a *Wolf Point Herald News* photo, standing at the group's edge. In the picture she looks fatigued, and is the only girl not smiling. She was silent on our trip home. When we arrived she slipped the dress onto a hanger in our metal wardrobe, and never wore it again.

＊

When at ten years old I read stories of the Little Rock Nine, I tried to place myself in the drama. I knew I wouldn't be the boy who loudly asked his teacher: "Are you going to let those coons stay in class?" I doubted I would join a "heel-walking committee" that followed black students through hallways, stepping on their heels till they bled. I pictured myself as one of the handful of girls who stealthily befriended the newcomers, or if I were grown up, as Grace Lorch, who sat beside a girl on a bus bench to protect her from a jeering mob after school.

Now I'm not so sure. I never once stepped between Rosemary and her taunters, though I didn't fear for my life. Even when I was strolling down the hall with Eva and Betty, friends I was sure of from merry-go-round days, I didn't stop to calm or divert Rosemary. I didn't want popular kids to link her with me.

Perhaps I was a kind of bully myself. At Make It Yourself with Wool, I hated how the girls glanced at me. So I made them admire me. I fussed with Rosemary's curls, softening their edges. I huddled with her over the printed program, keeping her on track. And when her turn came, I rose to guide her to the stage; from the corner of my eye I saw girls smile. I was oversolicitous and kind; did I think Rosemary didn't notice? She might have scolded me in precise diction: "It is inconsiderate to elevate yourself at your sister's expense!"

Rosemary never challenged my condescension. I thought that she was wise enough to grasp my superiority. More wisely, she may have understood the perils of challenging her one and only, though unreliable, friend.

Mrs. Gaustad is long dead. I'll never know what fueled her passion for the royal blue dress. Did she believe a well-made dress might heal Rosemary?

Why was Rosemary teased? My husband doesn't recall anyone so singled out in fourteen-times-larger Great Falls High. Are kids meaner in small towns? Or is there just not a large enough crowd for the oddball to go unnoticed?

Questions like these draw me back to my childhood home. I think that walking in my family's footsteps on our dirt paths will give me answers or relief. Rosemary and I liked to trail together down the long hill to the barn and chickens. Our thoughts were unspoken, though I longed to share my worries about her; perhaps she wished to voice her own. Might honesty have helped us?

The school bullies—boys whose names I remember—are grown now and graying. Most have moved away; they are salesmen, accountants. One of the boys, not part of the popular crowd, unathletic, sent a sympathy card at Rosemary's death. I ignored the card. He bothered Rosemary for a while in tenth grade. He hid her coat beneath another on the hooks, and one day took all the pencils from her study hall desk and threw them outside in new snow. Rosemary plunged bare hands down into slashes of snow for her pencils.

When Rosemary's two-dollar cartridge fountain pen, required for English, disappeared, my mother intervened. She seldom called the school, focusing instead on trying to change Rosemary, pleading with her and cajoling, as if she believed that normalcy lay dormant in Rosemary's brain, only waiting to be roused.

On a Saturday morning she phoned the boy's father at his town business. I listened from the living room; her voice was hesitant. The bullying stopped at once. When Mother died a few years ago, the boy, aged fifty, sent another card.

That's a mystery, but then so is having a sister itself. I still think about it, teased by the idea of a sister through Rosemary. Mother and Claire disagreed on politics (Democrat versus Republican) and religion (Methodist versus Mormon); still they wrote to each other every week for fifty years, and once sitting together in a car closed ranks against a child intruder. I could sit with a sister over tea (we did that), and muse about the future (we didn't have that chance). We could share secrets: Rosemary never told Mother and Dad how I might have killed us on the highway to Wolf Point.

Ginny

We would have a real baby in our house. Not just baby kittens that we liked to discover in the shed below our hill. We three loved kittens; even our mother would pause with her pail of fetid table scraps meant for the chickens, to clasp a kitten to her bib apron.

Most of our kittens would not survive, leading such perilous lives that our mother did not have to mimic Grandma's two-fisted drownings in the stock tank. Kittens were stepped on by cows and run over by trucks and tractors lumbering past the shed. Some lived to freeze in winter, or found strychnine-injected eggs left beneath the granary for skunks. Our dogs did not like kittens, though they tolerated cats at the fringes of our yard. One winter Bullet even shared his doghouse roof with mild Buttermilk; he licked her ear as together they viewed passing cars. A jigsaw puzzle-shaped piece of the ear froze and fell off.

The dogs seemed to ignore kittens tumbling in sunshine outside their shed. Then we might wake to find an entire litter dead, flung like rags around the yard, while our dogs grinned in satisfaction.

But a baby was forever. Mother announced the news to me in 1959 on a summer's day.

I wobbled beside her on my bike as she trudged between the chickens and the garden. I liked to follow my mother on her round of chores, plunging her hands beneath fierce hens in nestboxes, fumbling for weeds inside the slender shade of garden plants. Then indoors, shielded from the heat, I watched her rub manure off the globes of eggs, fingers nimble with a rag scrap. All that my mother did—beginning with the morning pancakes, ending when she rinsed the cream separator disks in the supper dishpan, shaking them on their storage wire like castanets—had a kind of weight.

Turning up the trail through the windbreak, Mother said, "I'm going to have a baby."

I tumbled over on my bike. When I righted myself, I realized that the conversation was over. I'd heard shame in her voice for having a new baby when we kids were entering our teens.

But I thought the baby was a gift, and Dwight and Rosemary did too, though taking a cue from Mother, we didn't discuss it. I added the baby to my prayers at night.

I prayed that the baby wouldn't have polio or be born dead. I didn't bother to pray against another Rosemary; I doubted there could be someone else like her. I wasn't really worried about the baby. I thought that the misfortune of Rosemary would ward off more bad luck: God wouldn't give us a second damaged child.

On a snowy March day I awoke to the milk pail's clang, the jingle of my father's overshoes, and the slam of the kitchen door. My father milked the cow at dawn but it seemed the middle of the night. I tiptoed to my parents' bedroom where the tiny headboard light shone on my mother, dressed in town smock and skirt and seated on the enamel pot. She stared at me, perplexed, as if trying to recall in what lifetime—childhood, high school, her carefree years as office girl— she had known me. My shock turned to pleasure: how important this event must be to transform my mother to a stranger!

It snowed all day, so my father met the school bus at the highway. He waited till the three of us had crowded into the pickup before announcing: "It was a girl." He delivered news, even good news, in a stoic way; his refusal to take pleasure was a strategy to ward off disappointment.

Rosemary and Dwight were silent; I kept my happiness inside too, waiting out the days until at last we tumbled off the bus to find our sister on the sofa in our overheated house. Mother looked proud. We took turns cradling her; Mother tensed when Rosemary held her in her clumsy way. After a few days Rosemary lost interest, but Dwight and I rushed off the bus each day to tickle and tease Ginny to make her smile. She had been thin at birth, and her skin blue. But the doctor hadn't seemed concerned, and after just a few weeks at home she became plump. I bragged about her blonde curls at school.

In July I accompanied my mother to Ginny's four-month checkup in town. I sat in the tiny waiting room, empty at field work time, paging through a magazine. I caught the eye of the pretty receptionist and smiled; pride in our new baby had lent me ease. Mother had also lost some of her shyness in town, smiling at women on the street who hurried over for a glimpse of our new baby.

Mother emerged from the hallway cradling Ginny in her yellow sunsuit. She dug a five-dollar bill from her purse for the smiling receptionist. When she turned, I saw tears streaming down her face. I followed her outside to the car where she said: "Ginny Dell's a mongoloid."

We drove in slow motion to the farm. For months we had been high on Ginny, our perfect baby, who diminished Rosemary's flaws. Our family had been on a kind of vacation from itself, our shame displaced by pride in our new baby. Now we were home again.

Mother stopped the car inside the yard, and I walked with her to tell Dad the news. He was tinkering with the tiny motor of the long-necked auger beside the windbreak. Mother began her tale. Ginny wriggled in her arms, squinting against the dazzle of the sun. I saw my father slump. I had made myself watch as a punishment: surely the arrival of a second flawed child had to be our family's fault.

Perhaps another family in another time might not have felt so ashamed of the diagnosis, which none of us went on to acknowledge in school, church, or town. Other parents, unweighted with worry and dread, might have hurried to the library to find the truth of Down syndrome's cause: a random genetic mutation. But in 1960 my parents weren't facing truths. They were facing another drought, one not as pervasive but just as deep as the drought of the 'teens that Grandfather Alexander documented in his diary. "Every little cloud is looked at with the wish and hope that it will rain," he wrote in 1917. That winter, hay was scarce:

> It is very noticeable how tired and worn out the horses are. They are getting dull, listless, staring, ambling. When hay or feed is brought to them they crowd up to the fence so close one cannot give them the feed. They fairly implore a person to give them something to eat. When a horse is called by name, he comes at once.

Grandfather tried to keep his livestock alive on "Montana alfalfa"— Russian thistle hay—but was forced to kill most of a double team of work horses: "Slim was alive but so far gone he hardly twitched an eyelid. I turned cows out, looked to the priming of the Colt, placed it close over the brain of the horse and pulled the trigger twice. Two reports and all was over. In three minutes Slim was being dragged out."

In 1960 my father did not shoot horses, but in August he did not grease the combine to begin harvest. Instead, each day I mounted Bud and moved our small herd into fields of shriveled wheat. A few hours later I hazed the cattle back into pasture again. Our crop was not worth wasting fuel to harvest. As we'd done before, our family would tighten belts, sell cows, and survive. Our area would remain in drought until Ginny's sixth birthday.

*

Before the doctor visit, I hadn't noticed Ginny's slanted eyes and bulbous tongue; I didn't think that Mother had either. She had wondered aloud about a single thing: that Ginny's head at two months still wobbled when she was held.

At home Dwight and I still liked to tickle Ginny, and Mother clicked her tongue to make Ginny smile, but in town something changed. Mother hurried down the street away from what she now viewed as prying eyes—women eager to carry back to Lutheran circles or the Women's Club their glimpse of Ginny's guilty face. Sometimes I lifted Ginny from my mother's arms and crossed the street as someone neared. I was proud to help.

Twenty years later on a visit home I strolled with my own baby on Main Street. Suddenly, Mother tugged me across traffic toward a woman who seemed startled, then smiled at our approach. My daughter was bald, no blonde curls, but the woman complimented her round blue eyes. As the woman edged away, Mother murmured, "I just wanted someone to see that she was normal."

At two years Ginny finally learned to walk; at three years she could barely talk. One night I decided to change that. I'd already gotten her through toilet training, thrilling my mother. Night after night I'd waited her out after supper, singing nursery rhymes as she perched on the enamel pot.

I settled Ginny in her little rocker near the living room's coal stove. When I was four years old I had lain awake all night (I thought) on Christmas Eve hoping for the rocker. Then I had sat in it beside the kitchen stove every day till first grade, eyeing Mother at chores.

Ginny smiled at me. She still hadn't figured out how to eat, scooping mashed potatoes with her fingers and slopping milk onto her shirt from a plastic mug. But I would teach her to talk.

Doing what others couldn't was the area in our family I'd staked out. I caught the horses in the pasture when my father stormed home without them; his impatience deflected them. Once, Minneapolis relatives called to say that they were in Dakota heading our way; Mother sagged as she replaced the phone. I tore through the house whisking furry dust off shelves, mopping every floor, and straightening the chore coats in their slumbering pile inside the kitchen door. As Frank and Effie's Nash Rambler nosed into our yard, I stepped outside with a last load of magazines for the burn barrel.

Ginny could talk, or rather make herself understood, but her speaking never seemed to improve. She clung to certain baby words like old favorites. "Yum" was milk. I pointed to a picture that I'd cut from a magazine: "Milk," I said. Ginny with her golden curls and clear blue eyes grinned at me. "Yum," she said.

"No," I said. Ginny still smiled. "*Milk*," I said firmly. "*Yum*," Ginny said. She chuckled at the game of matching me. Dwight and I played games with her that made us all laugh: lobbing an easy ball to her across the living room that she hurled back with all her might.

I shook my head and tapped the picture. "*Milk*."

"*Yum*," Ginny said.

In the kitchen Mother was finishing up her unvarying supper chores. She lifted dishes in a clatter from the rinsepan on the coal stove. Soon she would cross to the sink to fill the teakettle that all day long broke the silence of our house with its sighs and rattles. Then she would enter the living room. I reached out and slapped Ginny's cheek.

Ginny's mouth dropped open. She didn't seem to understand. But she was paying attention. "Milk," I said.

"Yum," Ginny whispered.

I was asking her to learn one small word. I could imagine the pleasure on my mother's face when she heard it. I slapped Ginny's cheek again.

Ginny stared. Then she buried her face in her hands and wept.

I froze. But Mother would not immediately appear; I heard the dull ring of plates being nestled on cupboard shelves. Ginny's sobs were muffled, though normally she cried long and loud when she was hurt, summoning our mother and her tender look.

I pictured Mother's look when she saw what I had done. She carried around in her purse an Ann Landers column with a poem, "Heaven's Very Special Child," which began:

> A meeting was held quite far from earth.
> "It's time again for another birth,"
> Said the Angels to the Lord above:
> "This special child will need much love."

Mother loved Ginny. But I knew love wasn't enough.

I'd slapped Rosemary in secret too. I thought her fits should be punished; discipline would rein them in. Mother only tried to reason with her.

Mother didn't like to punish; once I asked her if her own upbringing had been lenient or strict. The question seemed to stump her. Finally, she answered in terms of *Uncle Tom's Cabin*, which she'd read in high school: "I was like Topsy. I just grew."

I knew that my mother had grown up mostly alone. She was a 1920 afterthought following firstborn Dell—who died of an infection at seventeen; Claire; and babies born in '13, '14, and '15 who did not survive. Mother was scrawny at birth but lived, surprising her parents. Then my grandmother couldn't seem to interest herself in another baby, leaving the infant in care of older sisters while she toiled outside. In snapshots my mother—dressed in dungarees, blonde hair cropped short—is smiling, but she is always alone. Sometimes she clutches kittens.

I'd asked my mother the Topsy question because, in comparison to friends, I didn't feel raised myself. At recess girls complained that their mothers nagged them about chores and brushing their teeth: my mother washed supper dishes alone, lost in thought; I brushed my teeth when I pleased, often weekly. Sometimes in school I fabricated stories of harsh rules at home, inventing a new mother who kept a hawklike watch on me.

In the living room, Ginny had finished weeping. She wouldn't look at me. I heard ashes being shaken in the kitchen stove—then Mother appeared in the doorway.

She looked at Ginny's red face. Ginny had dried her tears, remoistening her sleeve's crusted milk. Mother stared at her across the room.

My mother wore her fearful look, as if she'd just received news of Effie and Frank hurtling across hot and dry Dakota to our door. That day she hadn't been able to think how to begin cleaning our house. Now she dropped her eyes to the mock carpet pattern of the linoleum. "Isn't it bedtime?" she said.

Mother couldn't acknowledge Ginny's hurt and fright; she had once also dismissed Rosemary's suffering. At age two Rosemary developed a fever, and was admitted to the Williston hospital. My parents left her and drove home. When they retrieved her after three days, Mother all but brushed off symptoms of her baby's distress at the separation, writing in her diary: "Went after Runty. Took eggs to trade. She'd pulled hair out and chapped lips but felt good."

Perhaps ignoring children's emotional needs didn't seem like neglect to my mother, reared largely by older sisters. Dell and Claire, bored with their chore, sometimes launched their tiny sister down a hill in her buggy while she screamed in fright.

Across the room, Ginny stared at me. I thought I saw a haunting in her eyes, a conflict of feelings. She did not know why I had hurt her; she wanted to tell our mother what I had done. She did not want to tell our mother; I was her best friend.

Neither of us told our mother the truth. I didn't slap Ginny again. The next day I was the recipient of one of her sunny smiles, though I saw a slight reserve. She seemed on guard, one of our family traits. I had made her one of us.

*

Ginny grew bigger, but she didn't grow smarter. She didn't start school. There wasn't any school to start; no one else around was like Ginny. Rosemary was slow in math and made trouble besides, but she was carried along by her superiority in reading. The only other Down syndrome child we'd heard of, and never seen, had been whisked at birth to Boulder River Training School five hundred miles away.

Ginny would be waiting when I stepped off the bus after school. "Horse!" she'd cry, and I'd drop my books and kneel for her to climb on. Then I'd rise and gallop through every room of the house, occasionally bucking, which made her squeal.

When I did homework in the living room at night, Ginny parked herself against the refrigerator door and dialed me over and over again on her red plastic phone, each time chuckling at my surprised "Hello?"

Then I left home, and only visited on school vacations twice a year. Ginny spent her days watching TV from her rocker and studying catalogs from which she occasionally snipped paper dolls. She accompanied Mother outdoors to the garden and chickens. At mealtime she served dessert, most times bringing in the pudding, cake, or Jell-O with an unconcealed grin, pretending to offer the largest one to my mother, then suddenly swooping it to Dad at his place.

When she turned nine, a miracle occurred: near the badlands of Glendive a hundred miles south, Eastmont Training Center rose on the rugged prairie.

All the state's institutions were in the west, where most Montanans lived: Deer Lodge Prison, hospitals for the insane and for tuberculars and lung-diseased miners, an orphanage, and Boulder River School.

Generous federal money was behind Eastmont. "Kennedy did a lot for the retarded," Mother liked to say. She had been thrilled to learn in his campaign of JFK's mentally disabled sister, another Rosemary. She stayed up late the night of the election, and at his ascendancy bought herself a fake fur coat. It was very cheap, inadequate for winter; its sad stripes suggested no animal I had known.

The president had been dead six years when Eastmont opened. Still, Mother credited to him the wonder of an institution that we didn't have to drive two days to visit.

Ginny moved at once to Eastmont, coming home on weekends by bus. She learned to make her bed. She had to eat mashed potatoes with a fork. Her speech improved with coaching from a real speech therapist.

Just once I detoured to Eastmont on a trip home. I found Ginny in the kitchen, stirring chocolate pudding on the stove. She had grown taller and wore glasses but was still plump with unruly blonde hair. She grinned at me, then at the counselor with whom she'd been sharing a joke. They chuckled; neither told the joke to me.

In her teens Ginny had occasional spells of weeping, a ghost adolescence. Once she snapped her eyeglasses in half for no reason.

At eighteen Ginny moved to Miles City, another seventy miles away. She joined five roommates in a group home, and spent her days in a sheltered workshop cutting old clothes into gas station rags and making paperweights of plastic molded over wheat. I didn't visit her but heard the news from Mother's weekly letters: she'd eaten pizza and gone bowling and camping; she'd learned to tread water in a pool.

None of which my parents had ever done.

She used earnings from the sheltered workshop to buy a stereo and wooden rocker. At Christmas and for two weeks each summer she went home; Mother said that she was restless at home. Once a group of birds made a racket in the trees, like shouts. Ginny rose and hurried outside in her clumsy way. She stood in the hot disked dirt of the windbreak looking all around for people in the low trees.

Long before my treks to the burnt-out farmhouse—where I would stand feeling slightly foolish, hoping not to be seen—Ginny also listened for voices in the wind.

Early one Sunday morning when Ginny was twenty-seven, Mother phoned. Ginny had been having "blue" spells, when she couldn't seem to catch her breath; she had a bad heart from birth, her doctor said. That morning she didn't wake up.

I drove alone to Miles City. I'd last seen Ginny two years before, when my family and I had braved the weather for Christmas at home. My daughter, Dell, five, and Ginny had played together on the floor of the mobile home, blonde heads bent over coloring, signing their names in awkward letters on the same page. They briefly argued when my daughter identified a snapshot's familiar face: "There's Grandma."

"Mama!" Ginny said.

At bedtime my mother invited Dell to sleep with Ginny in her room instead of on the living room floor. I opened my mouth to offer an excuse. "Okay," Dell said. It was Christmas Eve. An hour after bed I passed the room with Ginny's name in stick-on letters on the door. I heard voices and stepped inside. Beyond the window in the darkened room, a galaxy of stars twinkled. Two moonlit faces turned to me. "We're trying to see Rudolph," Dell said.

I arrived in Miles City to find my parents in the little funeral parlor, sagged in their chairs. Mother retrieved a funeral folder from her purse; on its cover was a field of wheat. Usually women's funeral folders featured praying hands or roses; men's had wheat. Did no one know where Ginny fit in? Perhaps Mother remembered that in good crop years she took pictures of us children in wheat. One wet year Mother snapped a shot of Ginny; she grins upward at Dad, who is trying not to appear pleased in belt-high stalks of wheat.

Inside the little folder I read the date of Ginny's birth, March 23, 1960, always *her* date; and now a second date forever hers: May 23, 1987. Below was her name—misspelled.

I flipped the folder over, and under Ginny's grinning face her name was spelled wrong again: "Ginny Alaxander."

I stared at the folder, a last token of Ginny. I knew that Mother would lift it again and again from her dresser drawer, studying the dates already burned inside her mind, the jarring name, to feel the presence of Ginny.

My parents sat with heads bowed, staring at the folders in their laps.

I remembered when Ginny was two years old I had stayed overnight with a friend in town, a rare treat. Eva and I made popcorn and watched TV; when we finally went to bed we kept talking despite her mother's regular pleas from her bedroom for us to pipe down. In the quietest moment of the night, when no cars passed, no dogs barked, I told Eva a secret: "Ginny's a mongoloid."

"Oh, yeah," Eva said. Her mother cooked in the hospital. "My mother told me that when she was born."

I lay awake stinging from the news. For months our family had displayed a perfect baby that I'd bragged about in school. But the town had known her defect all along. I tried to imagine the doctor—another in a series who soon fled our isolation—deciding at my sister's birth to delay the news. Was it my mother's timid face, her furled hair long overdue for a cut and perm, that made the doctor decide it didn't matter?

The funeral assistant appeared: blonde, young, about Ginny's age. He spoke, and my mother murmured thanks for his sympathetic words, then dropped her head. It would be my job to object to the flawed folder.

The assistant stood a little apart in his well-pressed suit, gazing at blue sky outside the window. I thought I saw boredom flick across his face before turning to us again. His eyes roamed the three of us: my father in his too-large western shirt—he liked the luxury of roomy clothes after a childhood in outgrown shirts and trousers, my mother's pantsuit in a dated gold tone, and me in a decent dress that I began to doubt as the man's glance swept over it.

I sat silent with my parents in our folding chairs.

The high, feminine notes of a piano reached us; we rose and filed into a nearly full chapel. I passed by stranger after stranger to our family's front row seats.

The service began; a minister intoned the Twenty-Third Psalm. A pretty young woman stepped forward to sing what she identified as Ginny's favorite tune: Debby Boone's "You Light up My Life." I tried to imagine Ginny, seated in her dark-varnished rocker, attentive to her stereo:

So many nights
I'd sit by my window
Waiting for someone
To sing me his song.

"You light up my life," the woman sang. "You give me hope." Did Ginny hope?

Mother whispered that all of Ginny's housemates were there: Richard, Marie, Andrea, Ann, and David, wooden in their row beside us.

Then the service was over, and our family stood together at the chapel's rear. My parents smiled and shook hands with the sheltered workshop director, a substitute counselor, a woman from the bowling lanes who served up cokes and fries. Richard, Marie, Andrea, Ann, and David lingered up front with their counselors where the pale blue casket remained. Richard and David were taller than their counselors. Richard was almost handsome; in high school he might have starred in sports. Classmates would shorten his name to Rick. I thought of the appealing names of all Ginny's housemates: how hopeful the new parents had been!

Suddenly a voice rang out: "No!"

Much of the rumble of conversation in the room ceased. "Yuck!" the voice announced; it was Richard's. Counselors moved in.

But Richard detached himself from the group to stand before my parents. "Ginny's going in the ground?" he asked. He hugged himself as if he were cold, though sunshine glimmered in the windows. He wore glasses like Ginny but didn't have a Down syndrome look.

"It's all right," Mother said. "It's what they do." She talked on, about how the real Ginny would go up to heaven.

"Will the hole get covered up?" Richard wanted to know. My mother fumbled to explain. She smiled at Richard. Listening to her soothing voice, I suddenly realized: I did not love Ginny. She was my sister, and I didn't love her.

I hadn't visited. I hadn't written letters or sent postcards or gifts. Now I noticed the large wristwatch sported by Richard; his hand groped toward it as he probed for more about Ginny. Someone had sent it to him; I knew Richard had an older sister. Did he feel a rush of warmth opening the gift while Ginny and the others gathered round? Had he fingered it before at last strapping it on to wear each day as a badge of his worth?

Not loving Ginny was something I had treated myself to, a way of warding off disappointment. I had been lonely for her when I left home, but I also felt the break as a relief. I wouldn't have to get snarled in her flawed life as I had with Rosemary's. I wouldn't have to lie awake at night stung by remarks and sidelong stares. I wouldn't have to search for improvement in her: no hopes, no fears.

No love. I imagined Ginny in her rocking chair beside the group home's wide window. To the beat of Debby Boone her mind sliding over the past, snagged by memories of our time together.

But Ginny had represented failure—ours or God's—that I thought I had an option to refuse. I had been glad to leave even small things behind when I left home: the chore coats' smell, the ancient teakettle with its slurry of hard-water scale.

Ginny had vanished; already I could hardly picture her. I looked toward the casket, where Andrea and Ann still hovered. It was so long ago that Ginny, as a baby, had lit my life. I wished just for a moment to be Andrea or Ann, tugged toward Ginny's casket.

✳

A few years later I happened to drive through Miles City, and on impulse parked my car before the Custer County Courthouse on Main Street. I walked up the stone steps to the cramped Clerk and Recorder Office in the rear, and asked for a death certificate. I didn't need to know more about Ginny's death; I just felt the paper was a last fragment of Ginny, something I should own.

It would be a while, the clerk—sixtyish, severe—announced. Death certificates were in the vault. An assistant scurried away.

The big book arrived, was clumsily balanced on the copy machine by the two workers, and the print certified with a hand tool. Then the clerk seemed reluctant to let it go, smoothing the sheet on the counter before me. She had sheltered Ginny, or her paper representation, in her vault for these five years.

Her face softened: "She was so young."

"Oh, it's okay, it's fine," I said. "She was Down syndrome."

The woman stared.

I went out the door and down the long oak hallway; by the time I reached its end I felt sick. Outside, I sank onto the steps. How many more times would I betray Ginny? I had shrugged off her death to a stranger. Seated on a corner of the stone steps, as feet pattered by, I wept for the loss of my sister.

I understood that I had grieved for her all along. My defective sister represented an accumulation of losses, beginning in childhood: the secrets not shared in bed at night, all our games circumscribed. Ginny and I had shared a single secret: my slap. All through her life there had been so many regrets spent, so many losses, that her death seemed hardly more than that: just one more loss.

I had loved Ginny before her birth, in my imagining of her, and in the years of her long babyhood. Perhaps I had not loved the blighted self into which she grew. But with her death I felt the broken link.

Now particles of memory are all of Ginny that remain, just as soon our family's farm will be only memory, though the land's shift from human occupation is unhurried, nearly imperceptible.

Normal

Rosemary would finally graduate from high school, one year late due to math trouble. The principal, who had not been unkind to Rosemary, mostly giving her a wide berth, was suddenly disturbed that in thirteen years no one had unraveled the mystery of her: the superiority in language, a math block, and her rage and loud laughter that had become fixtures at school. He made a pleading phone call to the hospital at Warm Springs five hundred miles away, and a few months later a psychologist arrived to examine her.

"She is a small, fragile-looking girl," the psychologist wrote in his report, "who looks almost mongoloid in her facial features at first glance but tends to be almost nice looking after knowing her for awhile." He persuaded Rosemary that his battery of tests might help her find direction following school: "She stated she was afraid she would do poorly, but she seeks to break the ties of her parents and to strike out on her own."

I did not read the report until years later, long after Rosemary left home. Our family received only a letter about the tests that I carried home in summer from the highway box. I handed it to my mother in the kitchen, out of sight from Rosemary, who regularly shredded into the coal bucket letters from school. Such letters often had a peevish tone: "I think it's just laziness," her fifth-grade teacher wrote as accompaniment to a march of math F's across Rosemary's report card. The letters plunged our family low; my parents were subdued at supper and at evening chores. They never replied to the letters or phoned the school. With no evidence to the contrary, we were locked in the notion that Rosemary was our family's fault.

When the psychologist's letter arrived, my father was in the fields; Rosemary was in the living room immersed in a stack of 1930s *National Geographics* to which Grandpa had once subscribed. Their photos of startled tribesmen and ads with swank men and women leaning on new roadsters were equally foreign to us.

My mother tore a strip from the envelope's edge. Over her shoulder, I read of the Wechsler Adult Intelligence Scale, the Graham-Kendall test, the Rorschach, then: "Brain damage is evident; chronic brain syndrome associated with trauma at birth."

I read the sentence over again, trying to let the words sink in. This was not just another letter from school. The bland bespectacled stranger whom I'd glimpsed at school had dug deeper into Rosemary than anyone else before.

A slight thing could set Rosemary off. On our ride home from Sunday School, if Dwight's *Sunday Pix* newspaper fell to the cramped pickup's floor and I accidentally stamped it with an overshoe print, he slugged me. I felt pain to the bone; then we forgot it. If I muddied Rosemary's *Sunday Pix*, she burst into tears and raged at me all the way home.

Then I hated her and sometimes indulged in a fantasy to soothe myself. I pictured her, like calves and the baby pig, wandering into the dam to drown.

The tests said that Rosemary's anger was not our family's fault; I tried to catch Mother's eye to share relief. But she tucked the paper back into its envelope and turned away. Dad also seemed to shrug off the letter when he scanned it at our noon meal: the mail never brought good news about Rosemary.

The psychologist wrote that Rosemary wasn't a candidate for Warm Springs State Hospital for the insane. She didn't belong in Boulder River School for the retarded: "Ability was quite high in the area of pure verbalness." He would look for institutional placement in progressive Minnesota.

Over a year passed that Rosemary spent restlessly at home. She sewed herself ill-fitting dresses of bargain percale. She sought to improve her speech, entirely banning contractions. She tried to train herself to eat with her right hand—fingers crabbed around her fork—as if it were left-handedness that set her apart. Finally, a letter from Minneapolis arrived in our highway box.

Rosemary could join a sheltered workshop and live in a supervised dorm. "It would be good if you could accompany her," the Opportunity Workshop counselor addressed Mother. Rosemary had never traveled; Minneapolis was six hundred miles away. But our parents dreaded travel in winter; on trips to Williston, Dad fretted that we'd freeze to death if we stalled, though the road was a main highway. Late one January night in 1967, Rosemary boarded the train in Williston alone.

Twenty-eight years after Rosemary's departure, and following my mother's death, I lift Rosemary's first postcard home from the stack of her correspondence saved by Mother in a greeting card box: "Had breakfast soon after leaving New Rockford. Dining car was 2 cars, so used gloves to open doors. Brr! Caught finger in door coming back from d. car. Arrived in Minneapolis and was guided through the residence by a Negro girl, Gwen."

The prose of her first missive, a template for all to follow, is meticulous; the portion of her brain controlling language was a triumphant survivor of the wreckage of birth. But where is Rosemary in this; wasn't she frightened on the trip alone? Surely her manner and home-sewn dress invited stares: "As we sat," the psychologist wrote, "she would talk in a loud voice as though she were shouting to the cattle in the fields." She must have wept when the heavy train door closed on her finger.

Rosemary was stamped in our Grandfather Alexander's mold. Through forty years of diarying, he dressed up mean homestead life in fine prose. His bleak, rocky farm was "Surprise Ranch"; winter's monotonous boiled dinner of stringy rooster was "another chanticleer in the pot." Lofty musings on his wife—who returned home only during school vacations—belied their rift: "A momentous day. In 1907 on this date I joined in wedlock to the finest girl in the world."

Grandmother Alexander was more plainspoken. In a note to Grandfather, which he pasted in his diary, she laid bare her objections to the farm: "Poor bed! Poor light! Run-down surroundings! Impossible to keep clean! No social contacts! No church! Poor mail service! Absolutely dangerous in case of sickness! No room for personal belongings! Space all occupied!"

Rosemary's prose masked hopes and fears that she had revealed to the psychologist, a stranger, whose detailed report was opened to me years later by the school principal: "She feels that her life has not been too meaningful up to this point. . . . She stated that others do not like her because she is 'different'. . . . She would like to be friends with everyone but is afraid of close contact."

In Minneapolis, Rosemary began life anew. At home she'd quit the Methodist Church in a crisis of faith; in Minneapolis she became Catholic: "Church is at 9:30, so must take pills, pin mantilla on & go!" At home she hadn't liked music; in Minneapolis she bought Johnny Cash records for the hi-fi in her supervised dorm. She volunteered to campaign for Hubert Humphrey: "She likes to discuss politics and appears to have an excellent vocabulary," the psychologist had noted. In April she remembered Mother's birthday, signing her card "Minneapolis Rose."

But her work at Opportunity Workshop, assembling and sorting, was geared for the developmentally disabled. "It is important to note that in the more academic-type tasks, this girl is functioning well into the high average range." Rosemary got bored on the job, then irritable; her counselor had to scramble to find new chores.

Rosemary began to arrive at work late. She clashed with others in her dorm. "She has experienced severe frustrations which have developed into anti-social patterns," the psychologist had observed. "I have not a roommate," Rosemary wrote home, her language still chaste of contractions: "Millie and I have had some disagreements."

Rosemary did not fit in. "She is the most frustrated person I've ever met," her workshop counselor wrote in his evaluation. But the counselor wasn't ready to give up. He thought she might live alone, and found a young couple to help.

Rosemary would move into the Iaconos' basement apartment. She had packed for Minnesota with a view of living on her own. On the typed list of her trunk's contents were dresses and skirts, "1 tight girdle," "1 string pink pearls," "1 string brown glass stones"—five necklaces in all—and "1 floral print apron."

She'd brought along recipes clipped at home for future use: Baked Fillets Thermidor, Skewered Lobster, Frozen Fruit Delight, Pears Helene. For her move to the apartment she bought *The Good House-keeping Cookbook* with promising chapter heads: "The Story of Meats," "When He Carves," "Vegetables That Say 'More,'" "Dreamy Desserts."

In her new apartment Rosemary plunged at once into Dreamy Desserts, making a fresh apple pie. It overflowed in the oven, sending smoke upstairs that brought the Iaconos down in a panic. She followed with a cherry pie topped by a lattice crust. Meanwhile, the Iaconos reminded her to flush the toilet and to bathe more often than once a week.

The Iaconos were aware of Rosemary's brain damage. They knew about her rural background, as described by the psychologist: "She is quite naïve and has had little experience coping with a general environment." Rosemary's country roots were reflected on Rorschach inkblots, where she had identified "a red-winged blackbird," a "Hereford cow," "two calves meeting," and "a freshly killed chicken with a severed head."

The Iaconos were unaware of the depth of Rosemary's privation, how our parents clung to a Depression-era frugality. Neighbors heated with propane; our parents stayed with coal, even cooking on a coal range. We were the last of the families on our school bus route to install a septic system, just a few years before Rosemary left home. Like our neighbors, also with alkali wells unfit for human use, we hauled water from town. Unlike our neighbors, my father hated to haul water in winter; instead we were encouraged to flush the toilet sparingly, and to bathe in shallow water once a week. Mother used a wringer washer, an early fifties relic, washing progressively darker-colored clothes in steadily dirtying water in the machine. When it gave out in the late sixties, our parents did not upgrade to the automatic washers sold in stores but found a mail-order replacement.

Weather often caused our crops to fail; our parents had to find ways to save. But good years or bad they scrimped, as if denial gave them pleasure.

At the Iaconos' house, Rosemary could learn to use fewer apples in a pie. But she could not get used to the gas cooktop that hissed and then exploded into fearful flame, or the washer-dryer set with its panel of confusing buttons.

Clothes went unwashed and toilets unflushed, but the breaking point for the Iaconos concerned their children. The workshop counselor had felt certain that Rosemary would find the small boy and girl a delight; instead, they irritated her. She was severe, scolding, as if the children's contentment was a grating reminder of all she had missed.

The living arrangement broke down, foreshadowed by the psychologist: "Some of her weaknesses are: her disabilities, her emotional fears, lack of social training and poor personal habits." Rosemary's next stop was a locked ward in downtown Hennepin County General Hospital, where doctors would decide her fate. A week later a notice arrived in our parents' highway box: "Petition for the judicial commitment of Rosemary Alexander as mentally ill."

Rosemary lost her freedom on June 18, 1969, a bright Wednesday, stepping into a car with strangers to leave behind the city that in two years had failed to deliver to her the gift of normal life. North of the city traffic grew light, passing through quiet country friendly with farms. The car slowed briefly on Anoka's Main Street, then outside town entered Anoka State Hospital's iron gates.

Thirty years later I visited Anoka, retracing Rosemary's route, though now State Highway 65 and County Road 10 are traffic-clogged, tortuous roads through sprawl that has transformed a town once twenty-five miles from the city into suburb. I passed through town and had to turn around again to find the small sign: "Anoka City Limits."

I found my way to the hospital entrance, no longer in the peaceful country. Under light rain I cruised the oval drive in my little rented car, eyeing empty buildings. Turn-of-the-century brick buildings—with 1909, 1911, 1913 carved in stone above the doorways—lined the drive, but Anoka had joined the decentralization movement of the eighties and dispersed its residents to community group homes. Through the whine of my wipers I identified one building as an office—a sign was taped to the window, cars outside. Another was a center for day treatment: young men in the drizzle, some of them smoking, eyed my slow moving car.

The towering buildings, ten or so, still seemed grand; I could be touring a college campus. I squinted into a porticoed entrance to my right and saw COTTAGE NO 4 carved in stone. Rosemary's nine-year home. I felt briefly in the presence of her.

Why was I hunting for Rosemary on this rainy day? I knew that this trip was extreme, not a day-long drive to our ghostly farm. I was seeking one more lost link—this time a tie to Rosemary—in one more abandoned place.

From my car I studied the sweep of drive. I thought of the men and women who had traveled the quiet road here during the long decades in which mental illness was more crime than disease. Had the towering brick uplifted them? Were the pillars and the roof turrets—still appealing to the eye—designed for the inmates' pleasure or to mask dismal lives within?

I would lean toward the latter when I read at home that as late as the 1960s inmates were buried in a back cemetery here, their graves marked only by numbered stakes.

The smokers returned inside, and I was alone in the rain. I looked at the buildings all around, still solid, and tried to imagine the generations of Rosemarys here with intelligence, five senses; equipped with sex organs that never found comfort, that on disabled persons are considered comical or hideous. Rosemary's mild cerebral palsy gave her abnormalcy away. But for how many others was it only something in the eyes—a fierce burning or a deadened gaze—that revealed illness? Except for some blight in the brain fruit, the people condemned here could have traded places with their keepers, some of whom must have spent most of their lives here too: bored, kind, or maliciously cruel.

Rosemary was admitted to the Social Rehabilitation Center at Anoka. She attended group therapy and took swimming lessons in the pool. A feature story in the *Minneapolis Tribune* identified her as the star reporter of the resident newspaper.

At Christmas she came home to visit. She remembered our family's birthdays, signing her cards "Anoka Rose."

She joined a Bible study group led by a town volunteer. At home, my mother had reported Rosemary's lapse in faith to the psychologist who tested her, approaching him shamefaced when we drove in to retrieve her after school. Everyone we knew went to the Methodist, Lutheran, Catholic, or Mormon churches. The psychologist smiled: "It's not abnormal to doubt God." Mother turned toward me stunned.

Religion did not smooth all of Rosemary's troubles at Anoka. "She is a very hostile girl, part of which is based on rejection," wrote the psychologist. Rosemary reported her difficulties in letters home: "It has been some time since I last wrote. Thank you for the paper. I have been in seclusion." A month later: "Last night Mrs. Roberts took away my books and records again. Things are fine here except for the above." And: "Yesterday, a young woman recently hired by SRC insulted me and I said, 'You're fired!'"

Rosemary began having seizures, and one year developed detached retinas in both eyes. That winter she visited me.

My husband and I had moved south for grad school, and at Christmas Mother made the surprising offer to fly Rosemary to us in Tucson instead of subjecting her to the long cold train ride home.

It was a first plane trip for Rosemary. I stood in a crowd at the exit gate, part of an excited throng waiting to search a sea of faces. Suddenly, Rosemary appeared on the ramp alone, a stewardess trailing. Rosemary had on a cotton dress that sagged below her knees; her face wore a troubled look. The crowd quieted. I stepped forward to claim Rosemary; the stewardess smiled at me. But I thought I could read in the stewardess's eyes: "she's crazy."

Rosemary gave me one of her open smiles, and I smiled back. She had ruined the holiday moment of finding a face in an airport crowd, and subjected me to stares instead. But I shrugged it off. The psychologist's report had helped me understand even her worst behavior: blowups that my parents at home couldn't reason away, that the school couldn't punish away. "Hostility based on rejection. Her frustration has developed into antisocial patterns." I'd been shocked to read that what my mother called Rosemary's "conniption fits" were fed by a view of herself as inferior. Her fits seemed to so energetically define her that I'd never imagined she might wish to be like us.

Still, as Rosemary ambled beside me to the luggage carousel, I felt cheated: my sister had been stolen from me. Had we lived somewhere else—not hundreds of miles from specialized doctors and psychologists—and without boys' bullying, teachers' scoldings, and my parents' blind neglect—might I have had that sister? "Few youngsters whom I have tested have been able to demonstrate learning ability in the area of general information that Rosemary has shown," the psychologist noted. "She has a very good chance of becoming a productive individual." Maybe he was wrong, dazzled by her *National Geographic* diction, or by her ability to answer a question three ways. Asked to define "domestic," she wrote: "a servant; being at home instead of a nomad; a pet, as *Felis domestica*."

While we waited for her luggage I saw that Rosemary was no longer a "small, fragile-looking girl"—she had gained weight. Her hair was cropped. She seemed drowsy or subdued. In a letter home she had listed the medicine she took: "2 white pills, 3 Dilantin, Synthroid, Akinenton, Phenobarbital at night." The hospital's recipe for cure? Or a cocktail to round off her rough edges for institutional care?

I picked up her blue cardboard suitcase that had belonged to my parents and lain dust-covered beneath their bed until Rosemary's departure. She shuffled toward the car. I looked down to see her feet encased in scuffed white flats, broken down, taking me back to childhood when we kids were allowed a single pair of new shoes each year at the start of school. I consulted with my husband when I reached home: we were on a student budget, but we could buy new shoes.

Early the next morning, I drove Rosemary to a mall store. I looked around at basic flats; Rosemary fingered canvas sneakers in a bargain bin. Then high on a shelf I spied a pair of walking shoes, of thick oil-tanned leather like our father's saddle. Their price tag took my breath away.

I had once believed in childhood that if Rosemary wore good clothes and shoes her oddness might be shrugged off. I gestured to the shoes. "Try those on," I said. Rosemary smiled. The clerk measured her foot and in the back room retrieved a box from which wafted a pleasant leather smell. He snugged the laces on Rosemary's feet; she walked across the room and back again, her gait improved. "Ohhhh," she said.

"She'll wear them," I said.

I do not expect ever again in my life to feel that much pleasure buying shoes.

One night my husband drove us around to look at Christmas lights, "Feliz Navidad" blaring on the radio. "A pity," Rosemary said on our return. "I'm losing my eyesight."

I checked out some books on tape from the library to help her pass the time; I found a Kennedy biography. She had been fascinated with the Kennedys in adolescence, studying photos of the clan with their handsome children, and drawing up a family tree. The psychologist had written, "She stated that she likes to read, and she enjoys paperbacks but she likes the 'wholesome variety.'" Rosemary listened to the tape with the same hungry look she brought to reading all day long at home. Then she was so absorbed that she didn't notice when she'd propped her feet too long against the living room stove in winter; we would shout at the smell of burning rubber.

Rosemary's Christmas gift to me in 1977 was a white embroidered baby dress. I was speechless; thoughts of a baby were years away. "I don't suppose I will ever marry," she said.

That morning Rosemary feasted on candy from her Christmas stocking, and fingered the gifts inside. Together we made cutout cookies as we did every year with Mother. But Rosemary and I stripped away the excess dough to eat instead of piecing it over and over again to make more cookies; at home our last batches were heavy and dense.

I thought I had given Rosemary a wonderful Christmas. On her last day I washed her clothes and folded them into the blue suitcase. "Would you want to take a bath?" I asked. Rosemary seemed hesitant. I ran a full tub of water, pouring in a capful of shampoo for bubbles. Rosemary shed her clothes and gingerly stepped in.

I was glad I'd gotten her into the tub. I didn't want to think about the old Rosemary who seldom bathed. Seated on the toilet lid, I asked if she would dip her hair back to be shampooed. She squeezed her eyes shut and let me tip her head. When she stepped out of the bath, I had her toothbrush ready with paste, and clean clothes in a little stack.

She left the bathroom and crossed the living room to settle in the overstuffed chair. She looked almost attractive, with shining hair, clean clothes. I felt proud. I felt as if I had created her.

Rosemary seemed exhausted from her bath. She gazed through the window of our duplex apartment, just dry desert outside. Then she turned and aimed at me a level stare.

I couldn't remember when she'd looked so piercingly at me, not even years ago when I'd lost my temper and slapped her.

Rosemary's eyes bore through me; I shrank in my chair. I thought that she was seeing my phony core. How the bath was for me, not her. How proud I was to buy her shoes. I was proud of myself for this visit—school friends admired me for devoting Christmas to a disabled sister.

Far back in childhood, when we had cut out paper dolls and murmured over play table teas, we had been equals. Now I treated her with condescension. "She has hostile feelings towards her sister, who is 'normal'": I had read the psychologist's entry in surprise. I had tried to best her in things, but only to prove to myself that I was not like her. I got good grades. I became a skilled rider; Rosemary was too clumsy to mount a horse. I even beat Rosemary in her area of baking, my steadiness mastering the tricky alternation of white and chocolate batter for our father's birthday checkerboard cake.

Rosemary still gazed fixedly. Then she dropped her head back and started to convulse.

I froze in my chair. My mind raced ahead to the kitchen for a spoon—I'd read up on seizures before her visit. But my limbs felt dead to my urging.

Finally, I roused myself from the chair; when I rushed back from the kitchen Rosemary's seizure was done.

She didn't turn to look at me but closed her eyes, sighing. After a minute I heard the steady breath of sleep. I tiptoed over and pushed back the handle to recline her chair.

Rosemary slept and slept. Dusk lowered; I kept a vigil across the room. I studied her. Even after our years apart, I could not see her fresh. I had never been able to see her face as strange, "almost mongoloid in her facial features." Everything about her seemed the same: her pale, delicate fingers; the slump of her shoulders; her light blonde hair, a color I'd always envied.

The next morning I waved good-bye to her at the airport gate. She strode purposefully up the ramp in her new shoes; I allowed myself to feel some hope for her. She turned to smile at me before disappearing; she had been put into a good mood by the ticket agent. "Too many Christmas gifts?" he teased about her bulging suitcase.

"HA HA HA HA," Rosemary laughed. "As though she were shouting to the cattle in the fields." Heads turned.

Rosemary arrived safely at the Twin Cities airport where no one met her. The hospital staff had forgotten her arrival, and neither Mother nor I had thought to phone ahead. Rosemary waited, growing anxious; finally, two nuns approached and made a call to the hospital on her behalf. "From now on I'll always feel good about nuns," Mother wrote.

Her letter with the news put a damper on my memories of the visit. What else had we failed to do for Rosemary?

"Rosemary considers herself different and inferior to other people and her family backs her in this feeling." I'd read this sentence in disbelief, in notes by the county social worker attached to the psychologist's report. He had dropped in before Rosemary's trip to assess financial need. Surely the social worker had got it wrong. Hadn't he gotten other details of our family wrong? My father wasn't five foot nine, but six feet tall. Our house wasn't heated by propane; a bucket of coal in the kitchen was in plain sight.

I remembered our family's reticence at his visit. We had a habit of ignoring Rosemary when company arrived, worrying that something we might say would set her off. Friends and neighbors ignored Rosemary, too, as if being polite.

Did the social worker not understand that our entire family felt "different and inferior to other people"? My parents were given two abnormal children. They worked hard but still could not get ahead: "The family has been hailed out completely the last two years," the social worker summed up his decision for need.

Only now am I shocked at what our family didn't do for Rosemary. We never visited her after she left home. In her nine years at Anoka, I never mailed a book or gift. Why didn't I send her a subscription, or another in the relentless series of Kennedy family biographies? She and I alike craved reading. When the *Ladies Home Journal* arrived in our highway box, I read it straight through, put it down, and later in the day picked it up again to study advertisements promising to cure nailbiting and bedwetting and testifying to the superiority of Klear Floor Wax and Lustre-Creme shampoo. Occasionally, our family was rich in magazines, when our grandparents found the drugstore's discards, minus their front covers, at the dump. Then for days our family sat silent in the evenings, drugged on magazines.

Mother, who sent me cookies just once after I left home, mailed Rosemary only what she asked for: "I hope that you can send some brownies, macaroons or fudge soon." In another letter: "Would you please send me six or eight *Fate* magazines as I have nothing to read except *The Clock Winder*, a novel by Anne Tyler."

In Tucson, Rosemary's suitcase was not swelled with gifts as the ticket agent presumed. I'd gotten her small things—socks, a dime-store watch, knit gloves. Her suitcase bulged because it was cheap.

Our family didn't buy gifts, considered frivolous, like praise. Now I imagine that other patients' families did. Right under Rosemary's nose other inmates received packages in the mail. Other families made the effort to visit.

Our family managed to make Rosemary second-class even in an institution.

✳

Four months after her Tucson visit, Rosemary, thirty-three, was dead. One morning she choked at breakfast: "asphyxiation due to seizure disorder," her death certificate read. Some corner of the dining hall, or of the world outside the window as spring was making new again, received a last fixed gaze; then she was gone.

A few weeks after her death, my parents got a letter from the Bible study volunteer at Anoka: "I just wanted to write and let you know how much I enjoyed Rosemary."

She was "cheerful and friendly," the Bible leader said: "Whenever we had her lead in prayer at the hospital, she always prayed a prayer of thanksgiving."

Even in her difficult life at home, she found enthusiasms; one summer it was cake. She pored over recipes in Mother's tattered cookbook, clumsily cracked eggs, measured and mixed. All summer squares of cake accompanied our pudding, applesauce, Jell-O, or rhubarb desserts. Rosemary made spice cake, chiffon cake, devil's food, and white cakes; topping them with powdered sugar frosting tinted bright blue, her favorite color. For hours after meals our family's lips were blue.

When Rosemary took up embroidery, Grandma Hawkins ordered her a subscription to *The Workbasket*; each month had a transfer inside. Scenes arose on our pillowcases. March's Easter bunny, basket in hand, strolled improbably through summer roses; a huge blue-bird—the design was for the first robin of spring but she liked blue—bumbled through a field of daisies. She learned the French knot, cross-stitch, lazy daisy, and satin stitch. When she ran out of a color of the five-cent floss, she couldn't wait for a trip to town, but changed in mid-flower—sometimes in mid-petal—to another color. Her clumsy fingers made the French knots bulbous; we awoke with their imprints on our cheeks.

One summer she began a collection of United States maps. She put a notice of her hobby in the reader's exchange of *The Dakota Farmer*; soon road maps filled our highway box. She became intrigued with Minnesota, "Land of 10,000 Lakes," long before she imagined she would ever live there. She counted the lakes. She thought she had miscounted, she started again, this time circling them on the map. "There are only 997 lakes," she announced in a querulous tone.

Mother tried to reason with her: "They just didn't have room for all those lakes."

Rosemary turned on Mother, her voice ringing out: "It is a lie!"

Mother persisted, always hopeful that reason could puncture Rosemary's mounting rage: "But it doesn't matter."

Rosemary gripped her shoulder: "You support their lies!"

A conniption fit was launched. Mother kept her temper throughout, her voice low, though with a note of exasperation as she pressed her case.

But the train of Rosemary's anger, set into motion, could not be derailed. She was shrill, weeping. The fight, unresolved, would finally die away when Rosemary's energy was spent. "Passive-aggression can be quite pronounced, and she is very capable of childish blow ups," the psychologist had noted.

✳

Recently, on what would have been her fifty-sixth birthday, I e-mailed Dwight. He had turned fifty-five the week before. I wrote: "I wonder what it would have been like to have a normal sibling."

Dwight replied that he'd thought of Rosemary during the day too. "I guess she taught us something," he wrote. "I'm not sure what."

I don't like some of the lessons that I've thought of. We three children were kittens, competing for the scarce commodity of parent approval. Farm litters often had a big kitten that nudged out the littlest one at the mother's teat. Sometimes the runt didn't survive.

Rosemary was that runt, lacking the charm or skill to gain a share of our parents' resources. I was a big kitten, attentive to what it took to suck most of the meager milk of parent praise. I memorized a thousand spelling words to become the eighth-grade county champ; in high school I studied long hours on my top bunk to be class valedictorian. I basked in Dad's beaming pride.

Once I learned the piano to please my mother, herself only a stolid accompanist to Dad's banjo. I taught myself from her childhood books, the *Bernard Wagness Piano Course I* and *II*, whose bindings were so precarious I had to turn each page slowly with two hands. Then we played duets, perched on kitchen chairs before the dark upright. I took the upper part; my grasp of notes was shaky below middle C. My shrill tones rose above her rumbling accompaniment. I deliberately galloped "The Little Postillion" fast, then slow; Mother collapsed in laughter.

Dwight soon withdrew from the competition. He spent his adolescence lying on dirt in our back yard, trying to coax a series of junk cars into motion. He didn't pay more than a hundred dollars for each, and wrestled alone with their inner workings. Dad, passing to the garage for a grease gun or outsized tractor wrench, did not stop to help. His son seemed invisible to him even when Dwight took up the challenge of restoring Grandpa Hawkins's 1929 Model A truck. Dwight swapped out the engine, replaced the old brass wiring, and even built a muffler of fiberglass tucked inside a corroded stove pipe. One of his cars—a smoking, blue '58 Chevrolet—carried him away after graduation.

My subdued parents, who were adequate to each day's chores but without ambition, and who adequately fed and clothed their children, but little more—were a generation trapped between adventurous parents and discontented children. Their generation's job was to hold on to the idea that hail-battered, drought-struck small farms could support a family. They awaited the next big experiment on the northern plains: the advent of large-scale farming. My generation left to prepare the way.

My parents' hold-on generation did their jobs well. They did not complain. They did not give in to fear and worry—nor to affection and joy.

*

Rosemary's last letter home was dated March 11, 1978, a month before her death. "Dear folks," she began in inch-high letters, her eyesight seriously failing.

She had good news: "I have a job now and have stayed out of seclusion since March 1st."

Her letter rode the hope of spring: "The snow is beginning to melt here and Allen Prill is looking at the seed catalogues. I am wearing the shoes that Ruth Ann bought. Give everyone my best regards."

I finger the letter, the bottom of the pile in my mother's greeting card box. Had I loved Rosemary? Not always. She knew how to ruin a perfect day. Even at one of my grandmother's dinners, over freshly killed chicken and abundant gravy, she could erupt. My grandmother's 1957 diary records such a visit: "Bill's came awhile. R. in a tizzy so left soon." I can still hear Grandma's voice with its Scandinavian lilt pleading, "Oh, Rosemary. . . . " But never entirely absent in Rosemary's life was her good cheer, which in her last years a polyglot of pills couldn't medicate away: HA HA HA HA.

We may have neglected Rosemary, but she did not forget us. Her last letter was signed: "Yours, Rosemary."

Would I have traded Rosemary for a normal sister? Almost always the answer was yes; now, as time passes, I'm not so sure.

I admire her stubborn spark, always dimmed by mental illness, that in an echoing dining hall at last flickered out. She had a willingness to engage others—she was less shy than I—and pursued ardent interests.

Her legacy to me is seeing the world through her eyes as an outsider, something I've grown to value.

She was often an aggravation. Outside our family, her life hardly mattered. I still miss her.

Haircut

I knew I was lucky to be Georgia's friend. I was her friend because I could make her laugh. Otherwise, I had nothing going for me: no money for clothes, no looks. But I could make Georgia laugh. Once in ninth grade when she looked across the aisle at me, I straightened into the stance of Teddy Roosevelt in our textbook picture, gesticulating as he delivered the speech about carrying a big stick. Georgia laughed. Then she wept. She had to get out of her purse a handful of Kleenex, digging around in lipsticks, chapsticks, two pretty combs, paraphernalia I admired. Georgia wasn't pretty, but her sister, a cheerleader, was. That Georgia's sister was a cheerleader, and also that she had the money for nice clothes and styled hair, canceled out what Georgia really was: a fat girl. I felt lucky to be her friend.

Georgia was always jolly, like a mascot to all the boys on sports teams and to the cheerleaders. At basketball games in the overheated armory that was our gym, she milled around the cheerleaders after the game, waiting with them for the players to come up from the basement showers all decked out for their dates. I watched from the stage where the pep band had played, drawing a swab through my clarinet. The boys said things to Georgia that made everyone laugh all around before slipping away in the frosty air with their dates.

Georgia ignored my cheap clothes. I tried to keep up on hair, though my curls sprang out of their pageboy. Most of the other girls had perms, out of the question for me. But with natural curl I didn't need it. At the end of school each year Mother hacked my hair off Dutch-boy style; by the beginning of school, it was long enough to roll under again into a pageboy.

Then at the beginning of my senior year something changed. A cheerleader (not Georgia's sister) came to school with hair cut short, layered in soft curls. A razor cut, she called it. Everyone gathered around. Georgia and her sister got new haircuts and perms right away. I thought Georgia's face looked even rounder with her short hair.

All the girls started getting razor cuts. In our small high school no one was a stranger; when anyone came to school with a new haircut— usually on Monday morning—girls who had already cut their hair gave even freshmen knowing smiles.

Once a year my mother got a haircut and perm in town. But it was a necessity: Mother had the straightest, awfullest hair, as she often said. By the time of her April birthday, limp curls reached almost to her shoulders. As her hair lengthened, so did the row of bobby pins Mother used to keep it from her face. On April 29, her birthday, we were all glad when she came home from her trip to town alone, with new short hair in a knotty perm.

But I had curly hair, fine-textured, in a nice shade of brown. From articles in *Ladies Home Journal*, I identified it as my "best feature." Even when it sprang out of its pageboy into curls, Georgia admired it. When we loitered in the school's basement lavatory after lunch, waiting to rush to class at the insistent buzzer, Georgia liked to take a comb from her purse and run it through my hair.

After her razor cut, Georgia no longer dug around in her purse after lunch for her rattail comb or the large pocket comb to draw through my hair. She rearranged her new curls at the mirror. I waited beside her for the bell to ring, listening to the sighs of leaking toilets. Georgia finished her hair and smiled at both of us in the mirror.

I didn't dare ask for a layered haircut in town. I knew how tight things were. On Saturdays, when we drove to town for supplies, I followed behind Mother on her snail's pace through the grocery aisles. It was shopping by rejection: not ketchup but mustard, not real vanilla but the imitation, everything else off-brand.

My only spending money came from occasional babysitting for a well-to-do Missouri River rancher. One late night I craved a snack and opened up a cupboard door. The contents of the cupboard seemed strange; the rancher's wife didn't bake, at least not biscuits, muffins, cookies, cake, pie, and bread, as my mother did. I looked for crackers in the cupboard. At home I could have all the saltine and graham crackers that I wanted. I ate saltines and grahams on alternate days; sometimes for a change I put them together in what I called a brown-and-white sandwich.

At the top of the cupboard I spied something we never had at home: hot dog buns, cozy in their plastic bag shaped just for them. At home we had hot dogs often, minus the bun. And the ketchup. I pulled the bag down from the shelf just to look at it. I saw that two buns were missing—why not one more? I worked a bun free; unlike Mother's bread, it was feather light. I decided to sneak a look in the refrigerator for ketchup. It was right in front, tall among milk cartons (the ranchers didn't have to milk a cow). I twisted off the cap and laid a band of ketchup all along the bun. My mouth watered. Suddenly, I heard a sound and turned to look into the wide eyes of a six-year-old: "What are you *doing*?" I crushed the bun in my hand and scooted the little girl back to bed.

After the haircuts began, there was a change one day at school. We switched seats in typing class because Mr. Grissom couldn't see the faces of some of the shorter kids in the room. I was moved behind Candace, the cheerleader who had started razor cuts. We had four cheerleaders, the royalty of our school.

We had lots of down time in typing class. Mr. Grissom explained that we could learn as much about typing by reading our manuals or studying our keys. He hated racket.

The typing tables were narrow front to back; students sat close. Right away I stared at Candace's hair. I knew she wouldn't turn around and catch me, someone beneath her radar. In the long boring minutes—Mr. Grissom said that he wouldn't start a time test till the hour, and suggested that we practice typing in our minds—I studied Candace's hair.

I broke it down: layering meant that all the hair was the same length. About three inches, I gauged, moving my pencil dangerously close to a blonde curl.

"Begin!" Mr. Grissom shouted. Fumbling my fingers onto the keys, I missed a few precious seconds of the one-minute test. I crashed through the test, making mistakes that I knew would dearly cost me: three words subtracted for each mistake. But I was jubilant. I had gotten Candace's hair. Then at the end of the test, Candace turned her head to gauge her progress on the wall chart. I had time to memorize the side of her hair down to its jaunty spit curl.

On Sunday afternoon, in front of my mother who was baking, I removed one of Dad's razor blades from the cupboard above the kitchen sink. I went to look for the tape to cover one sharp end. I also found the scissors in their drawer.

The tape, the scissors. Ours was a household of single things. Also "the chapstick," and, until this last year when I had used babysitting money to buy my own, "the hairbrush."

In my bedroom I squeezed myself into the space before my mirrored chest of drawers. I pushed back my little figurines—puppies and kittens ranging in play all across the chest of drawers—and removed Goldie, the goldfish, to a safe place on the floor.

I'd already washed my hair in the kitchen sink, and stood ready before the mirror. Dad was outside doing chores; Mother was still baking. I picked up a reed from my clarinet. I'd thought the discovery that my reeds were three inches long a good omen.

I stood the clarinet reed on my scalp and drew up a hank of hair— about six inches longer than the reed. I sawed with the razor blade at the reed's height, and the hair fell off. My haircut had begun.

Piece by piece I cut my hair, watching myself in the mirror. I carved off long strands, each releasing a curl that tumbled forward on my scalp—perky and pretty. I wondered if that was how Candace felt every day: perky and pretty.

Hanks of hair drifted onto my crowded cat and dog figurines. Some fell on the floor beside Goldie, who darted around her bowl in the excitement.

I kept waiting for trouble. But in a little over twenty minutes the part of my head in view looked as good, I thought, as Candace's.

Then it was time to move to the back. I parked the clarinet reed on my scalp and looked into the mirror. The reed and the hand that held it had disappeared behind my head.

I gripped the reed that was trying to slide down the slope of my head, and lined up the razor by feel. I sawed, and a hank of hair fell onto the floor. A tingling arose in the tip of one of my fingers.

I set up another strand of hair. The second stroke of the razor sliced across my thumb. I took my thumb down to look at it. The cut was across the joint, which resisted bending. I went out to the cupboard above the kitchen sink to find a Band-Aid, feeling a little rising panic.

The house was quiet. Mother had absented herself outside in chores. She had glanced at me when I took the razor blade, freezing in mid-stroke as she pushed muffin batter into fluted paper cups. I gave her a broad smile; she didn't need more worry.

I wrapped the Band-Aid tightly, numbing my finger, and picked up the razor blade again. I went on. I cut, blind, row after row across my head, cutting my fingers repeatedly. I switched hands, sawing at strands of hair left-handed. I cut myself immediately and switched back.

I cut and cut, settling into the feeling that the blood and pain were normal, the razor's cut a not unpleasant stinging.

At last I was through. All of the hair I could feel was short. The curls in back weren't perky, but matted and sticky with blood.

I doubted that Mother was in the kitchen, but I couldn't take a chance. Kneeling beside the tub in our sinkless bathroom, I rinsed pink water from my hair.

Before it was dry, I wrapped bunches of hair around plastic rollers, securing straggly ends with bobby pins. I had no idea what I had done.

*

From her sentry post on the school's front step, Georgia spied me stepping off the bus. Everyone mingled before school began, and Georgia liked the top step to pick out friends to greet. I saw her mouth drop open.

On the bus ride to town I'd tried to get used to my new hair, touching it with my fingers. I couldn't feel it through the bandages and it worried me. What if it was awful? Though I didn't think so. Mother's jaw dropped when she saw what I had done. As I pulled the rollers out before school, she said it looked fine; she tried to look at the hair instead of the bandages. Four of the fingers on my left hand and one on the right wore bandages.

"Kid!" Georgia shouted. "It's cute!" Others turned to stare, but Georgia was smiling. I walked closer, waiting for the smile to fade.

Georgia squinted all around my face. Finally she said, "Who cut it?"

I looked at her. It was a normal question; she did not look horrified. I tried to smile. I was waiting for her to make the connection between my Band-Aids and my hair—hacked fingers, hacked hair—but suddenly Georgia disappeared, ducking to view my hair from behind.

In the silence as Georgia stood behind me, I promised God that if I could get away with it just this once, I would never again try to cut my hair.

Finally, I heard Georgia say from behind: "Vicki?"

Vicki—the youngest, prettiest hairdresser in town! Not the one Mother went to. I felt Georgia fluff my curls and smiled as she faced me again.

But she was studying the Band-Aids and at any moment she would guess. I decided to give her a hint, as if I wanted her to know. "My favorite hairdresser," I said. "Very exclusive."

"Shirleyann?" Georgia asked. Then she named the only other hairdresser in town, the one who cut my mother's hair: "Louise?" I shook my head.

Just then the big orange Dane Valley bus rumbled into view. "Oh, honestly," Georgia said. She was smiling at the mystery of my hair or at someone disgorged from the bus. "Oh, never mind."

I watched my best friend drift off.

Had she guessed, I decided, I would have told her. But I would have spun it into something to make her laugh—as though it were hilarious even to me that I had become my own hairdresser.

That day in typing class Candace turned her head all the way around to look at me. We were between speed tests.

My haircut was so late that she had already gotten hers trimmed up once. She stared at my hair, then at my bandaged fingers. No one had yet remarked on the bandages, looking like a suicide gone berserk. Candace looked all around at the hair on my head, at our matching spit curls—then she smiled.

It was the first time she had smiled at me. It was the first time I had looked her in the face. I saw she had tiny freckles across her nose that she probably hated.

I had practiced the confident smile I would return if a cheerleader ever noticed me. Now I saw a little light of friendliness in Candace's blue eyes. We were nearly twins in spit curls and shirtwaist dresses. Candace's dress was blue, highlighting her eyes. Mine was a woven red plaid with brown tones the color of my hair. My secret was that, for a fraction of the cost of Candace's dress, I had sewn my own.

But my hands were rough from outdoor work; I wore imitation suede leather shoes, balding. In 1964 the country-town divide was real, breached by a handful of rural families who prospered. The ranchers for whom I babysat had inherited their sprawl of bottomland beside the river. A few farmers found off-season jobs, and some drove school buses.

My parents were not among them. They led their own parents' lives: my father waiting out crop cycles, Mother raising much of our food in a large garden, and saving eggs and cream to sell in town.

What else divided us from the others? My parents were shyer than most rural neighbors. My mother had stayed home six years after graduation, performing office chores in town, then after work hoeing potatoes, riding the binder to cut wheat, and shocking corn. On every third homestead or so in our little valley, a child had not left home. Often the youngest boys helped on the farm till their parents died and they took over: Roland Forsyth; Howard Nelson, the tallest of the Nelson bunch, considered slow; Windy Piercy; Dennis Blair. A few years after I left home Dennis Blair, sixty-two, had been dead perhaps a week when a neighbor dropped by. He found Dennis in an easy chair before the booming TV on which he liked to watch an afternoon soap.

My grandparents did not coerce Mother to stay home. They did not discourage her rare night out, such as to the dance across the river in

Sioux Pass Hall, where she met Dad. But they did not challenge their timid child's reluctance to depart: the workload of homestead life trumped their instinct to push a fledgling out.

Candace, who did not rise at dawn to board a bus but walked a block in soft snowboots instead, smiled at me across the dark varnished table in the high-ceilinged room. I could not smile back.

"Begin!" Mr. Grissom shouted. Candace turned around. I hurled my fingers onto the keys and banged hard. Pain shot up through the bandages. I didn't care. I hit the keys hard enough to murder them, and at the end of the minute I had to count my words twice. With the ringing of the machines still in my ears, I found that I had typed ninety-three words with only one mistake: a new top score.

As the class watched, Mr. Grissom lengthened my red line on the chart with his colored marker. I had passed Candace, the queen of our typing class.

In the lavatory following lunch, Georgia resumed combing my hair. She liked to plump my curls with the handle of her rattail comb, sometimes removing the little mirror from her purse for me to admire it. I tried to keep us talking while she did my hair. I didn't want her to start wondering about my hairdresser. We talked about boys—which ones were cute. I deferred to Georgia's judgments because of her associations, though neither of us had ever had a date. We talked about what teachers were cute. I cracked her up by trying out her name with Mr. Grissom's—"Georgia Grissom." I said he'd saved himself forty-five years just for her, though he hadn't managed to save much of his hair.

Georgia laughed and laughed.

Each day I kept my secret was a triumph.

Then I broke my promise to never cut my hair again. Christmas, and our holiday concert, loomed. My curls were drooping, dangling. I set aside a Sunday afternoon for an experiment. From Mother's closet, I dug two mismatched church gloves from a pile of discard clothes on the floor. I slipped them on, and readying to cut, I studied myself in the mirror. My left-hand glove, holding up my hair, had a tiny row of fake pearl buttons. I looked like one of the models in my mother's magazine: ladies who dressed up in gloves even for visits to the hairdresser. But I had to abandon the gloves—one pale pink, one white. My hair slipped in them, making my cuts jagged.

The remaining school year I cut my own hair. On a Sunday afternoon I arranged my tools on the cleared chest of drawers as if for surgery. I found a better technique. I prebandaged my fingers, dulling—but not altogether omitting—the razor's slash. I hated to waste the bandages.

Through the rest of the year Georgia stayed my best friend, waiting for me on the front steps, or just inside the door in frigid weather. She started wearing lipstick, making her look slightly clownish. In the high-walled lavatory she tried it on me: I couldn't smile back at her in the mirror; with dark red lips I thought I resembled my mother.

Georgia never asked who cut my hair. I believed I had fooled her.

Candace never smiled at me again.

*

Thirty-five years later I reconnected with Georgia, managing to locate her with just a first name. "Oh, everyone knows Georgia!" the small-town grocery clerk said.

Meeting up, I felt once more in her shadow: in our years apart she'd had two marriages, one heart surgery, and met Elvis.

A Seattle friend had been the Elvis link, an off-duty policewoman hired for security at his 1970 concert. She'd sneaked Georgia backstage where they bumped into Elvis in his sequined suit; he invited them to his dressing room.

Elvis didn't try to impress them with his life but inquired about theirs: where were they headed that night, and what would they do? What kind of parties did they go to? He couldn't just have fun anymore, Elvis said.

Georgia told me her own wistful tale. Despite a happy-go-lucky air in school, she had nursed a secret sadness, a parallel to my family's poverty that I worked so hard to hide: she had lived in the shadow of her older sibling.

Her mother couldn't accept an ugly-duckling child, and pressured Georgia to lose weight and acquire the boy-magnet charm of her pretty sister.

Georgia and I at last shared our secrets. Long ago, close as we were—intertwining our fingers as we waited in the hot lunch line—we kept them inside, following the pattern of parents and grandparents. They had learned in a harsh country to imitate prairie grass: keeping their most vital parts deep and protected underground.

New immigrant Kyrle Hakkansson, my maternal
grandfather, age sixteen, 1896. Before heading west,
he anglicized his name to Charles Hawkins.

Wedding portrait of my paternal grandparents,
William and Mary Alexander, July 31, 1907, Morristown,
Minnesota. William, age forty, was Morristown's superintendent
of schools, and Mary, twenty-six, taught first grade. Six years
later, William moved his family west.

Grandfather Alexander shingling the roof of his new homestead shack.
Snapped by an itinerant photographer.

Rosemary, Dwight, and I pose for
a picture on the front steps
following baths, 1951.

My family on a visit to the Hawkins farm, 1954.
Left to right: Me, Dwight, Bill (my father), Norma (my mother),
and Rosemary.

Me with the milk cow's calf chained in the backyard, 1955.

Our house following a late spring snowstorm, 1961.

Charlie and Ella Hawkins at home in
1963, in front of the 1904 log house
built by Charlie.

Ginny and my father in tall wheat, 1972.

My parents in 1986, nine years before my mother's
death, inside an Amtrak train on their single trip to
visit Dwight in California.

Bomb

My grandfather had his accident when he was eighty-five, on a sunny spring day I had to waste in town at high school. He was walking at his age-defying pace through the pasture when he spied a cyanide bomb in a hole. It was the last of a bunch he'd set out years before, as soon as he heard of them through the county agent. Then he decided that the cost and danger were too high, something my father had said all along. The little device was waiting for a fox to trigger it, injecting itself with a pellet of cyanide.

Grandpa Hawkins in his overalls and blue chambray shirt stared at the bomb in the hole. The others had exploded years before, most in foxes, though a few had given mega deaths to gophers instead. Grandpa decided to dismantle it. He was not sure how to override the action, but after all this time could it even still be dangerous?

It was.

Dripping blood, he strode the cow trail home, taking a shortcut through the soft disked dirt of the windbreak. In the house, my grandmother lifted the teakettle from the stove and poured it over Grandpa's hand in the washbasin. The water turned pink. Grandma grabbed a dish towel from the little drying rack above the stove and wrapped his hand; she went to find her purse. She was an infrequent, timid driver, and so short she had to peer above the pickup's steering wheel. Grandpa shook his head; she didn't even need to ride along.

Grandpa started the pickup left-handed, and turned right on the highway for the seven-mile trip to Culbertson. Two miles short of town, Grandpa passed out and entered the ditch. After a minute he awoke, started the pickup, and maneuvered it back onto the highway. In town he managed to coast to a stop outside the doctor's door. The doctor glimpsed the blood-soaked towel and summoned his nurse to drive Grandpa to the hospital; he would soon follow. Grandpa shook his head. He started his pickup again, and delivered himself four blocks away to the hospital.

I did not know about it until hours later when I stepped off the bus from school. Mother stood in the kitchen looking helpless. Dad, in the fields, hadn't been told. I changed out of my blouse and flare skirt into an everyday shirt and jeans and ran a half-mile to the field. I stood on the edge of the dark plowed dirt and waved, managing to interrupt my father's absorption in the seed drill. He finished his round and stopped the tractor, engine convulsing. I shouted my news.

Though my father and grandfather farmed together, they often clashed wills. Dad disliked Grandpa's enthusiasms. At eighty he had self-diagnosed his lagging energy: "It says in *Taber's Medical Dictionary* in black and white," he told us, "that the cause of pernicious anemia is lack of hydrochloric acid." The town doctor refused to write him a prescription, so he mailed away for a thousand gelatin capsules that he filled from the gallon jug of hydrochloric acid he used in his machines. Dad was silent as Grandpa fumbled for a capsule following meals. But one day when I hiked up to the harvest fields with afternoon lunch—cookies, cake, coffee, weak Kool-Aid—my father in the pickup shade gestured out of sight behind the combine where Grandpa had stepped for some relief: "He's draining his batteries." Because my grandfather did strange things and made mistakes—he wasn't a rock-solid adult—I sometimes felt closer to him than to my parents.

I finished telling the story of the accident to my father who was studying the neat contours of the seedbed. Just one more field and the machinery would be moved to my grandparents' place, Dad lumbering it over prairie hills. He shook his head. "Nothing to be done," he said. He released the clutch and the big orange Case rumbled forward.

When I got back home, the hospital had phoned to say that Grandpa's time was short; could Grandma be brought in? My mother, a timid driver like her mother even in our one-stoplight town, looked imploringly at me. "Someone has to stay and milk the cow," she said. "You like to practice driving—"

I'd had my driver's license for a year but only driven a couple of times alone; mostly I ferried Mother on trips to town. I slipped into my skirt and blouse again, and backed our new car, a seven-year-old blue-and-white Chevrolet Delray, from the cramped garage, and turned down our gravel road to the highway. I'd only driven inside our yard before taking the driver's test in town. The patrolman, so handsome in his uniform beside me that I trembled, gestured out the window with his notebook as I crept down Culbertson's main street: "You're on the wrong side of the road."

Rounding the first curve toward town, I glimpsed the towering blue spruce of Grandpa's windbreak. "His blessed trees," Dad scoffed. Grandpa had even tried to grow fruit trees, foreign to our extreme climate; only crabapples with their puckery fruit thrived. Cherry trees turned black the first winter. Two woody vines survived a mild year to produce a handful of rock-hard grapes. A pear tree lived four years, bore a single fruit, then died.

I turned up the little lane and parked outside the stucco house, mounting the stacked railroad ties of the front steps. Grandma was standing in her crowded kitchen dressed for town, her cotton house-dress and bib apron swapped for a rayon jersey frock in a pattern of indefinite swirls. A belt was clasped across her round middle where a waist might be. Entering her kitchen, I always felt high hope. Beginning with the ringing jangle of her screen door, I felt myself step into a world slightly altered from my own. She baked heavier cakes than Mother that I believed I preferred. I even preferred her papery saltines, beyond stale in their high cupboard shelf.

My grandmother stared at me, then shuffled past and into the car, carefully arranging her cotton-stockinged arthritic legs. She was silent, gripping her purse as I followed the circle around her prairie yard and through the trees again. We looked up together at the tallest tree, closest to the snow-collecting highway ditch.

I turned west onto the highway, where there wasn't a car in sight. But all around, scattered on low hills mounting toward the horizon, were farms I knew. I knew their cars and the colors of their tractors. I knew the names of their horses, and whether they were tame, and if they grazed in pastures with Hereford or Black Angus cattle.

I crept down the highway at my grandfather's speed. Beside me, Grandma didn't speak. I missed her sing-song voice naming things.

I thought of Mother, who had thrust this job on me. At this moment she sat milking, ducking beneath the milk cow's tasseled tail that swished overhead lifting flies from her bony back where they would settle again. I felt proud that I'd swapped milking for a grownup's chore.

My grandmother peered at Howard Nelson's farm along the highway. Our tall Norwegian bachelor neighbor—"High Pockets" my father called him—whom we often met going to town on Saturdays in his faded green Chevrolet, had died of cancer just this spring. I stared at the small house absent now of Howard's litter: coils of old fence, a possibly useful metal gate, a stock tank he meant to solder, and a retired sickle mower—skeletal—always reminding me of Howard himself. All gone, carted into a pasture coulee by out-of-state brothers, leaving a naked house.

Grandma stared straight ahead. Outside seemed emptier when she did not inhabit it with her gaze, spotting minute changes in weather and in farm details. I glanced at her dress, a favorite for church, and at her feet encased in moccasins with slits cut out for swollen toes. Grandma seemed entirely familiar: her cellar smell, scabbed hands. I had lately become ashamed that she and Mother did something that I could not: plunging their hands beneath hens in nestboxes to retrieve eggs, ignoring the tattoo of sharp-beaked pecks on wrists and hands.

Suddenly, I felt tired and realized how tightly I was gripping the wheel. I was still a nervous highway driver. I looked at my grandmother, sparrowlike, shrunk in her seat. She still had not spoken. I felt a tiny flicker of resentment toward Mother, who should have been in my place in the car.

At home she would be finished with her chore in the fly-infested barn. The cow, freed into the corral, would be drowsing.

I looked over at Grandma again, at her dress pattern of dizzying spirals and felt an urge spring up. I had never driven the car above sixty, my father's speed, but something had changed. My grandfather's death was certain. I stepped down hard on the gas.

For a second the car hesitated—as if it doubted its ability to follow through—then it rocketed forward. A wind sprang up outside the window. From the engine a whine rose as if raising an alarm. My grandmother still sat wooden.

I thought I could get beyond the engine's whine; I pressed the accelerator to the floor.

Outside, the detail of wind-tousled grass vanished. On a hillside, horses stamping at flies blurred. The speedometer needle whipped wildly. I had entered new territory, driving faster than anyone in my family had before. I looked down to see the needle pass eighty-five, the highest number on the gauge, and point to a gray zone.

The body of the car began to shudder. As my grandmother sat lumpish beside me, I thought of my grandfather. The speed and dissolving landscape made me feel close to him, to the intensity and excitement of his approaching death.

The engine whine became steady, menacing, like that of our dogs before they lunged at a visiting stranger. The car's knocking grew louder, the steering wheel began to tremble in my hands; suddenly I was seized with fear that the mounting racket meant the car was about to disintegrate.

I lifted my foot from the pedal just as I glimpsed, in bright spring grass at the highway's edge, a set of tire tracks turning into the shallow ditch and disappearing.

I saw, indelibly, my grandfather. His flash of gold tooth—which made my father declare he was worth more dead than alive. His funny

Swedish accent—everything was "dis" or "dat"because he couldn't say "th-" Talking politics with my father after one of my grandmother's Sunday meals, he called our country's menace "da Rooshians."

I peered along the highway but couldn't see the tracks where he had driven onto the road again. The car drifted toward town, tires whispering. I coasted past Bowers's coulee, deep, tree-lined, where Grandpa's pickup would have overturned after tumbling in.

I was beginning to feel what it would be like to have my grandfather broken from my life.

I drove slowly through town to the hospital at its far edge. Beyond the isolated building lay pasture and a field, then the cemetery. I heard the chuckle of a lone tractor in the field.

It was supper time; only a single vehicle was parked outside the door. Pulling near, I saw it was my grandfather's, a 1955 black Chevrolet pickup, bought new after two good crop years. My father had bought the same pickup; ours was sky blue.

I parked a little distance from the pickup. My grandmother peered around me. The truck seemed unhurt by the ditch accident, maybe dustier than before. I couldn't help staring at the round, bright eye of hubcap on the nearest front wheel, turned inward at a crazy angle.

Walking to the door, I slowed my pace to my grandmother's. At five foot five, I towered over her. In sixth grade I had felt ashamed to reach her five-foot height, a trespasser in the adult world.

A nurse watched our approach, swinging open the heavy door for us to enter. She led us down the single hallway past mostly empty rooms; from a bed someone craned his neck to stare. She halted outside a vacant room. "It doesn't look good," she said, "but the longer he goes on—." She shrugged.

My grandmother sighed.

I blurted: "It's in God's hands."

The nurse, and my grandmother in her rimless glasses, turned to stare at me.

The nurse led us down the hallway to a room where she tiptoed in. My grandfather seemed to be deeply asleep. His chiseled face below tousled white hair looked normal. But his breathing was labored. Each exhalation had a sound, a long sigh somewhere between weariness and extreme satisfaction such as followed a Sunday meal.

When the nurse had gone, Grandma murmured, "My mother sounded like that."

I knew that my grandmother had lost her mother from pneumonia when she was just six, after a fall through river ice.

We settled ourselves on folding chairs. An hour passed. I was embarrassed that I'd mentioned God outside of church. But I'd begun reading the Bible, searching for clues to my future soon to begin at graduation. I wondered if I should go far from home, or to junior college in Williston an hour away.

Suddenly, the nurse appeared in the doorway with an invitation: Grandma could spend the night with a former homestead neighbor, a widow living in a house in town.

I got back into the car and drove in slow motion through the streets and onto the highway again. Outside town I passed Bowers's coulee; the dark trees seemed full of knowledge, foreboding. I looked hard at Howard Nelson's house as I passed by. In addition to the Bible, I'd started studying the landscape for clues to my life ahead, trying to see if familiar places would tug at me to stay. But the sun was low, its dazzle gone from Howard's windows; they stared at me blank.

The car no longer seemed new. Though its engine hummed and the plastic seats smelled fresh, I believed that I had damaged it. I thought again of leaving home, going far away. I hadn't yet told my parents that I dreamed of leaving farming, its dirt and manure and worry, the monotonous cycle of seasons. But I wasn't sure what else there was outside of farming. What could be as huge as farming, which occupied most of my parents' thoughts and hours every day?

I'd changed since summer. Before summer, Aunt Claire in California had suddenly married a Mormon widower with seven children; two girls were the ages of Dwight and me, instant cousins. Our few real cousins were older and far away. Claire had brought the kids out in June for a visit.

We hurried over to Grandma's when they arrived. We found the girls, in bright shorts sets, perched on the bed in Grandma's spare room, staring out the tall window. Nadean, the oldest, said, "What is there to do here?"

I didn't know how to answer. If she couldn't find interest in all that was outside—a long prairie yard leading to the windbreak; beyond that a pasture with hills, rocks and flowers, startled rabbits, watchful cows, and a coulee junkyard whose discards were a timeline for all my grandparents' years here—what could I say? I'd never been bored at Grandma's.

Over two weeks the cousins began to enjoy their visit. I felt as spoiled as a town kid with company each day. We taught the girls how to wade through knots of chickens, dissolving them in a nervous flutter, and to edge close to wary cows. Dwight and I held no sway in the adult world, but we enjoyed dominion over animals. Even my father's horse, Bud, obeyed the slap of my reins as well as Dad's, though once at age nine as I saddled him, Bud shifted and stepped onto my canvas-shoed foot; I felt it drive into the soft ground like a stake. Then Bud acted merely annoyed, twitching an ear, as I screamed and pounded on his muscled shoulder. At last he moved; I limped for a week on a foot with a quarter-moon-shaped purple bruise.

The girls never learned to like the prairie junkyard. They stood at the winding coulee's edge eyeing a binder that had cut and bundled wheat for threshing in pre-combine days, the pretty icebox with nickel fittings, an open-air jalopy. They recoiled as if this really was junk instead of receptacles of time.

Now I think that the junkyard I visit not far from my parents' burnt-out farmhouse may one day be the single testament—if the new owner strikes more matches, and as grass creeps back, overtaking fields—that my family once lived there.

✳

Driving home from the hospital, I passed my grandparents' farm, silent beyond its dense rows of evergreens. My grandfather, arriving here from a country that was two-thirds trees, was shocked by the bare plains; he had to drive a team seven miles to the river for cabin logs. He soon began his own forest. And behind his house—I glimpsed it as I passed—was a fortlike stack of wood, discarded railroad ties he'd hauled home from beside the tracks. They were useless, too bulky to build with, too creosote-soaked to burn, but the towering pile remained.

At last I turned up our road, and entered the yard to park inside the dirt-floor garage. I knew I would not tell Mother and Dad about my driving.

In bed that night I awoke twice, believing I heard the telephone ringing news of my grandfather's death. But all around was silence.

I thought of the darkness and silence outdoors. I was afraid of the dark, something I couldn't tell my parents. Occasionally, I was sent late at night to shut the chicken house door. Just a little jaunt down the hill, familiar chickens peered worriedly from their roosts. But returning home I was terrified. I wasn't afraid of coyotes, foxes, skunks, or porcupines, but of darkness itself. I felt something lurking that might spring out, as my thoughts, unbidden, came forward at night in my cramped bedroom: boredom with my parents' life, imaginings about the handsome patrolman.

Since summer I hadn't been able to forget the fun of our cousins' visit. The four of us pulled stunts that Dwight and I would never do alone: while grownups gabbed indoors, we took Claire's car out of gear and pushed it halfway down the road to the highway.

And I couldn't forget the day that Cheryl, the younger one, came over, and we set out on an aimless walk, following the road to the highway, crossing a low pasture and mounting the railroad grade. We headed west on the high tracks, stepping across wooden ties snugged in crushed rock. We talked about high school and friends. We talked about our mothers, so unalike. Cheryl said it was hard getting used to a new mother. Suddenly, we looked back to see we'd hiked a mile, one-third of the way to our grandparents' house, a distance I'd never walked before. We decided to surprise everyone, and ambled on. We strolled that sun-washed morning on the high railroad grade above fields and prairie. On the bright band of highway alongside, a few cars passed; some of the drivers slowed to stare up at us. Then Dwight showed up below. Mother was unnerved by our disappearance, so he'd fired up a junker and set out. Dwight reported that Mother guessed we were following the tracks to our grandparents' place; she had already phoned ahead. Cheryl and I instantly changed plans, swearing Dwight to secrecy. Let them assume we were headed to Grandma's; we'd turn around and walk back home.

I felt such happiness that day under the blue dome of sky. I wore cheap black sateen shorts bought just for the cousins' visit, and a home-sewn red bandana blouse. I felt happy to have a friend, but more than that I felt happy to be free of my parents. They didn't know where I was. I was in slight trouble, worrying my mother. I wasn't my father's trophy-grubbing daughter.

Months later, as I lay in bed awaiting the telephone's insistent ring, the pleasure of my cousins' company still seemed fresh. I knew I had to leave home; since the girls' visit I'd felt lonely on the farm. But would anywhere else in the world ever feel like home? Grandpa Hawkins had crossed the ocean at sixteen never to see his home or family again. How had he wrenched himself away?

I thought of my grandmother, who had knit herself to her farm in a way my family hadn't. We named cows but not favorite chickens, which were mock-scolded by Grandma as she waded through a sea of them to find eggs in their low-ceilinged house. Grandma even named the "jails" in which she locked hens to break their habit of sitting on their eggs to hatch them; the crates were "Bismarck" and "Fargo," after bustling North Dakota towns. She named her highest field north of the house bordering Indian land "Pikes Peak." I was in the upper grades before I was certain that the Colorado peak was not named after hers.

How had she linked herself to a land whose promises of health and wealth were so unmet? I sometimes sifted through her early letters to her future husband in Montana: "What fun you and I will have chasing over the hill. We can play like little children, and in the summer fish and hunt. Oh! Won't it be great to be Mrs. Hawkins!"

The letters did not sound like her later daily diary that I also liked to browse through: "Cleaned more in corral. At 10 I started to bake—not done till 5—bread, pie, 2 cakes, chicken. So tired."

On May 1, 1957, two weeks past her seventy-first birthday, she "cleaned 1 room chicken house, 11 tubs, so tired. I wish I was a horse."

I still puzzle. This country hollowed her out, snatching three babies when the work was too hard during her pregnancies, and taking merry teenaged Dell when a hospital was too far away. Did she transfer love for her lost children to the world around her? When we strolled outdoors she called out names of things like a caress, drawing herself closer to the harsh country that had taken from her so much.

Morning at last arrived. My parents rose early, then stalled at breakfast. Mother wondered if she should make a phone call; she hated to disturb anyone. She worried that someone was on the party line; twice she rose, lifting the phone from its cradle to hear the bland buzz of the empty line. My father, always rushed at breakfast, stirred his coffee and watched as the sun rose through our kitchen window, heralding a perfect day.

The telephone jangled.

Mother answered. "Oh!" she said.

My grandfather had awakened at the hospital impatient to go home; he had to fan more wheat for seeding.

In a week Grandpa Hawkins did get home, and when in another week the bandage was removed for good, his hand was not the same. The doctor had not attempted amputation, believing that Grandpa would not survive. But he had dug around in the palm before giving up, extracting bits of muscle and flesh in which cyanide might be dissolving.

My grandfather lived eleven more years, still active, at last taking to bed with a flu from which he did not recover. He wore a winter mitten on his hand even in summer; his hand felt cold, he said. The mitten covered up the hand's gouged-out useless look. Grandpa learned to eat with his left hand, to drive, and signed his checks with a childish left-hand scrawl. He was cheerful about his hand to curious neighbors when he finally returned to church. He had been missed; at our small church fewer than two dozen members spaced themselves apart on dark-varnished pews. Filing out afterward, everyone chuckled as he showed how he could shake hands with the minister as well as before, using his left hand.

My grandfather would never admit his foolishness of trying to disengage the bomb. Grandma, out of habit, was mum. The event was fodder for several mealtime ravings on the part of my father, who called it a perfect example of what he ran into working with Grandpa every day. Mother tried to wear a neutral look that didn't betray her husband or her father.

For a few days at school I basked in the curiosity about my grandfather's foolish deed, though at bottom I thought it was more adventurous than foolish. So did the little group of seniors in study hall, all of us counting the days till we were done with school, possibly forever. I described the explosion of the bomb. My grandfather's lone trip to town, driving into the ditch and out again. He had barely survived. The seniors listened, gazing out tall windows to the high, blank sky.

I didn't tell anyone about my high-speed driving, how I could have shared a death with my grandfather. A few months later I left home, crossing the state to the university six hundred miles away.

Leaving Home

At 4:00 A.M. my mother didn't have to wake me; I had been listening in the dark for her first stirrings. I slipped off my bunk and fumbled into my new pleated skirt and matching top.

In September 1965 I was bound for the university in Missoula, though Dad was only sure that he could pay for one year of school. Mother wondered if I needed college at all: "You'll just get married."

My father rushed out to milk the cow, who was surprised to be urged into the barn before dawn. We ate a breakfast of my mother's flat-but-delicious pancakes—she cut Bisquick in with plain flour to save bucks—then Dad changed to Levis and a western shirt and plucked his wide-brimmed hat from its shelf. It was 5:00 A.M.; we would have at least a two-hour wait for the nine o'clock train in Glendive, a hundred miles away. My father's worry over being late was something I was glad to leave behind.

In gray light my father backed the car from the garage. "Good-bye," I said to Mother. We didn't hug. She didn't speak. I closed the front door softly; outside was a little wavering breeze. I got into the car and waited while Dad loaded my trunk and three new red suitcases. I looked up to see my mother at the kitchen window. Framed by tangled curls, her eyes were wide.

Dad slipped into the driver's seat; as we pulled away I realized I hadn't said good-bye to Bullet, whom I would elaborately hug and kiss before even short trips to town. I caught a glimpse of him inside his cramped doghouse peering curiously at me.

It was not yet dawn when we reached Culbertson. Past the slumbering town, Dad turned south and crossed the narrow bridge of the Missouri River. Beyond its towering breaks of fissured sandstone and shale, the land settled into the rough country that Grandfather Alexander had homesteaded, where my father had spent his youth. The soil was thin, road cuts exposed rock, buttes rose. Dad studied the buttes as we drove by: the cluster marking Three Buttes Ranch, and the twin spires of Sioux Pass—so named, he said, because Indians had used it as a lookout for bison. The stories of Indians and bison hunts here seemed unreal, like a child's game.

Dad was silent as he drove. I knew that my parents didn't want me to go six hundred miles away to school. No one else in my class had; of ten college-bound classmates, I was the only one to travel far. Most of the rest were heading to teacher and technical training in Havre or Billings, 250 and 300 miles away.

Dwight—who couldn't seem to get far enough from home, soon shipping with the Marines to Vietnam—had encouraged me. It hadn't been a hard sell. Our parents were not part of the warp and woof of the community. We seemed to be the only family related to no one except grandparents—all the fault of my parents' siblings who did not stay here and marry.

I'm still learning through the Culbertson paper how many families are linked. Before a recent school reunion, I was surprised to read in an obituary that two women my mother's age—who'd married into separate large families—were sisters, and that one of my classmates was their niece. The next week I saw Sandy at the reunion banquet, catching her on the fly as she hurried to greet new arrivals in the school gym. "Are you related to everyone in Culbertson?" I joked.

"Just about!" she called back gaily. Sandy had gone to junior college in Glendive following graduation.

Fifty miles from home, Dad and I neared Sidney, the town he had moved to at seventeen, leaving his father's dryland farm for a two-month job trucking sugar beets in the vast, irrigated Yellowstone Valley. Sidney seemed foreign to me, luxurious with trees due to irrigation. I pictured its people leading lives far easier than our own: the trees absorbing wind, summer heat, and winter blizzards.

As the sun burst over low hills, my father cleared his throat and said, "These have been your formative years."

I stared ahead, startled by Dad's first acknowledgment of my leaving. Last night I had finished my picture album, gluing photo corners into which I slipped black-and-white snapshots of me with kittens and with Bullet, and astride my horse Goldy, who had never liked me and whom I'd never managed to tame. I ordered myself to write inside my album cover when I returned at Christmas: "My Formative Years."

I felt a weight from my father's pronouncement. I wasn't sure I wanted to believe that my childhood was done, implying that the chance to fix some things was over. I would never be friends with Goldy. Nor would I ever have the mother that I wanted: the television kind who gave hugs and kisses, and who threw big birthday parties— instead of cake with the family after supper—and who shooed me into adulthood with the injunction to aim high.

I would have liked that mother; still, I felt a tug toward my memory of the startled face in the kitchen window.

We beat the ticket agent to the Glendive station. When he arrived to open up and check my luggage, Dad's good-bye was brief. "You'll make it," he said. "Trains don't run off the track much. Hang onto your ticket."

I could see he was anxious to hurry off, concerned about the trip home. Good weather or bad, his anxiety away from home stayed constant, on calm days summoning old dreads and stale worries as stand-ins for real threats of weather.

Inside the train I sat carefully on the pleats of my black-and-white-checked outfit's skirt. I'd packed a sandwich in my new straw box purse. When the train at last lurched forward, I thought that my body had been poised to receive the jolt for a long time.

After awhile I heard young voices above, and climbed up the short steps to the Vistadome, where I found a seat alone. Across the aisle three dark-haired boys playing cards looked up at me and to their game again. They began to horse around. They had been on the train awhile, and were friendly with a serviceman and a couple of older girls two seats behind. In the banter I picked up that the boys were from Chicago, and also on their way to the university. I wished that I weren't invisible to them.

A porter entered, perfectly black in a perfectly white suit, bearing oranges in a basket for sale at ten cents. I checked the urge to spend my money. One of the boys joked with the porter, then announced: "Everyone in the car gets an orange on me!" The three boys convulsed in laughter.

The black man lifted a pale palm and chuckled softly; he began to dispense oranges. I accepted one and peeled it with a sinking heart. The porter's guarded laugh and the boys' glee was a transaction I could not fathom. I felt my anticipation sag; I would be out of my league in Missoula.

Already my clothes were wrong. The black-and-white-checked skirt and top set from the Aldens catalogue was too dressy, a contrast to the boys' knit shirts and rumpled trousers not even new for school. I would be more certain of my mistake in Missoula when sixtyish Aunt Mary, who had agreed to ferry me from the train to the college dorm, remarked, "You'll get a lot of use out of that little suit."

Eating my orange in the Vistadome, I felt lonely. These were my new classmates, and they seemed as exotic to me in manner and dress as former Sioux Pass Indians. I should have gone to college in Havre or Billings, havens for small-town and rural kids. I doubted that a single Chicagoan had set his sights on those schools.

That evening on campus I moved into a shared basement dorm room with matching twin beds—but I was not a twin to my roommate, blonde and statuesque. I thought I saw her face fall when I walked in. She left almost at once for a Coke date with new friends.

I unpacked the trunk and three suitcases, carefully hanging up my new pleated skirts. They were another Aldens catalogue find. A yard of pre-pleated material came with a finished waistband; one had only to cut the material to length and sew on a waistband and button: all for about half the usual skirt price. The pleats weren't very full, and the skirts—dark blue, light blue, dark red, and brown—were checked like my skirt and matching big-buttoned top. I hoped that checks were in fashion, but I hadn't seen any so far.

I changed out of my new clothes. I had left behind my "everyday" clothes, a shirt and ill-fitting pair of slacks that I slipped into each day after school; last night I had shed them like snakeskin onto my bedroom floor. In my new room I tried to relax in "town" shirt and jeans.

I was continually startled by glimpses of myself in the closet mirror, I'd gotten my first real haircut from Mother's hairdresser the day before, her last appointment of the afternoon. I was proud to be initiated into beauty shop culture—with its gleaming tools and chemical smell—by the smiling hairdresser. But something made me feel small, like Mother's comment about college wasted on women headed for the altar. Why hadn't I deserved a haircut before?

Over the next few days in Missoula, I found my way to classes and to the feastlike offerings of the dining hall. My roommate surprised me by passing up breakfast; she worried about her weight, though she was feather-thin. At lunch and dinner I stuffed myself on soda pop and salads, never served at home; I finally had to move my skirts' waistband buttons. I drank pop just a few times a year, when Dwight and I rode with Grandpa to Williston for machinery parts at harvest time. At the Co-op Grocery he invited us to choose a treat. Dwight and I plucked warm cans of Shasta soda from the store shelf.

I was amazed when a boy in the dining line slammed a fist onto his tray at discovering that the main course was once again meat in thin gravy. I liked all the food, as I had liked all our food at home. I wasn't crazy about Grandma's fall parsnips, or a kind of dark bread she bought in town, but I ate them anyway: if I did not like a food the blame was mine.

Once a week I wrote Mother, telling her about meals and my Sunday attendance at the Methodist Wesley House; I concealed from her that in my new home I felt a stranger. My mother answered me at once in letters dense with farm news: the chickens were laying well for fall; she'd seen a weasel streaking from their nestboxes in midday. Bullet missed me; her mention of him was a surprise. She'd never minded Nip—accidentally killed last year by Dwight's jackrabbit start-up in a car—but something about Bullet's stupidity or his all-black ugliness annoyed her. She didn't trust him. She thought he stole eggs from the chicken house, and convicted him on a guilty look. When she came up the hill with just a few eggs clutched in her apron, she asked: "Have you been eating eggs?" Bullet dropped his head and slunk away.

My sixth letter from home arrived with its typed page outlined in black crayon. Bullet, aged ten, on a routine lope alongside Dad's pickup heading north to the upper dam, had suddenly dropped dead.

During the first months of college my skin dried and flaked from every-other-day showers. We had no shower at home; I'd never seen one until our family's vacation to the Black Hills in South Dakota. Dwight and I hadn't been able to stop showering at the Lariat Motel in Deadwood; we showered in the morning and at night, and again if we came back to rest in the afternoon. Finally, our mother couldn't stand it. As if the water were directly drawn from our backyard cistern three hundred miles distant, she forbade us to shower more than once a day.

Our vacation, during the 1950s wet years, was my only trip away from home. Dad sprung the idea on us the day before. Dwight traced the drive, which would consume half of our days away, on a gas station map. I dug out a vacation checklist from the pile of *Ladies Home Journals* beside the couch. The list wasn't very helpful. "Stop milk delivery" was #3. Dwight beside me, ten years old, said, "Guess we'll have to shoot the cow."

We didn't have to pack much into our parents' battered black suitcase because we all wore the same clothes for three days.

In Deadwood, Dad ignored Mother's worried look and treated us to our first ice-cream sundaes. He beamed as Rosemary, Dwight, and I stood in awe of Mount Rushmore's giant faces. Following the trip, Dad never overcame his dread of travel again. But even the short vacation, I was sure, had prepared me to leave home. I didn't get homesick at all, not even when someone mentioned—and every day at five o'clock one of us did—that right now Grandpa was milking the cow. Arriving home, I scrambled onto my bunk to thumbtack a tiny Black Hills pennant to the wall. I felt myself a confident traveler.

✳

That fall at school I didn't have a period for two months. I knew I wasn't pregnant; I'd never had a date. Recently, I read that malnutrition or the stress of war can halt menstruation. I wasn't malnourished, though I'd begun to limit myself to only six cups of orange or root beer soda per meal.

I wanted to cry most of the time during the first two months, from the strain of the unfamiliar, and because I hadn't made new friends. I kept looking for a twin, a fellow eastern Montanan, but they were few. One I met seemed like Dwight, wanting to put as much between herself and home—represented by me—as she could manage. After a few weeks I made myself a rule: I could cry only once a day, in the morning when I had an hour alone. I looked forward to the ritual. Entering the dim basement room, I removed my blue-striped bath towel—the father of its little matched family—from the rack beside the sink. We hadn't towel sets at home; this one was a gift from Mother bought with Gold Bond Stamps, one book. Lying on my bed with the Gold Bond towel pressed against my face, I sobbed. I took breaks to check the time. When the hour was up, I hung the towel back onto its rack to dry.

I signed up for a humanities course, and learned I'd have to write a paper. I hadn't written papers; in senior English, *A Tale of Two Cities* was followed by a multiple-choice test. For our first paper, we were asked to describe Odysseus's heroism in *The Odyssey*, an epic poem I'd had a hard time reading through.

I was intimidated by the classics, but I liked the course. Part of the appeal was youthful Mr. Dunsmore, who with his gentle manner and perplexed frown was unlike any man I knew. Once I had to rush from class as the bell rang, straight to the women's room where a Wesley House acquaintance found me crying. I struggled to explain. Mr. Dunsmore had announced that he wasn't Christian. He found the religion, employing pagan symbols, interesting, he'd said, but he wasn't a Christian himself. "Oh, I know!" Karen gushed. Her eyes shone. "We're meeting so many interesting people at school!"

I sobbed, "But he won't go to heaven with us!"

In my dorm room I pondered the hero question. I was afraid to write a paper, and more afraid to displease Mr. Dunsmore, about whom I'd begun to fantasize. Then an idea came to me with such clarity that I imagined it was what Mr. Dunsmore hoped we would all write about. Odysseus wasn't a hero at all. His men were the heroes; they didn't talk and dream and dither; instead they sailed ships, roasted whole oxen, and risked their lives in savage battle. A week later, near the end of class, Mr. Dunsmore pulled our papers from his briefcase. He had something to discuss before returning them, he said. Then—a dream come true—he began to read my paper to the class.

The students sat rapt. I heard my earnest voice combined with Mr. Dunsmore's making my case. He read my summary, strong praise for Odysseus's weary men, then dropped his head. Mr. Dunsmore's frown—never about scanty June rain or the government's price support for wheat—deepened. "This paper is quite well-written," he began. My heart crashed in my ears; he regarded me as his intellectual twin; we would someday marry—"but the assignment was not to attack the entire Greek myth of heroism in a two-page paper." I went numb. When the class finally ended, I darted outside and down the hall.

In the women's room I was surprised to see a B-minus on my paper, along with strong cautions about the topic, and writing praise. Mr. Dunsmore had given me a lingering worried look as I stumbled from the room, making me wish I'd ironed my checked skirt the night before. After just one wearing the cheap pleats relaxed, resembling rolling hills of my homeland instead of sharp mountain peaks of my new town.

In November I quit crying. My period returned. When I had given up on meeting someone like me, I found a best friend. Cynthia was from Butte, where her father and brother worked deep in the open-pit copper mine that regularly swallowed workers, and whose borders constantly enlarged to swallow the town. Cynthia's family had moved once when the pit reached their home.

What had we in common? Cynthia had never visited the long plains of the east or lived on a farm; I had never been to Butte. But her hands were chapped like mine, and her fingernails bitten. She had my habit of changing clothes when she came home from class, carefully slipping skirts and blouses onto hangers to preserve them. We didn't speak of it, but like me she felt the strain of school. Cynthia stretched herself too far. Forcing herself to major in chemistry, she flunked out in spring.

In December that first year, I took four finals and managed to collect Bs; then I boarded a train for home. At Glendive I got into an aging van that served as a bus to Sidney, Culbertson, and a few more points north.

I'd brought my copy of *The Odyssey* to read on the trip, partly to calm my inside churning—the feeling that I'd like to rush as fast as I could back home. Or did I want to rush as fast as I could back to Missoula?

The van was crowded; children in heavy coats squirmed on parents' knees. A serviceman beside me studied his cigarette's orange glow. He was about my age; I wondered if he was also returning from far off. He looked at me and smiled; I turned away. I hadn't yet begun *that* kind of education at school.

Not until after Christmas would I begin to date, going out a few times with a Wesley boy to whom I poured out my life story and my angst over Mr. Dunsmore's sure descent to hell. The Wesley boy just wanted to kiss.

Dorm mates would engineer a blind date with a boy who informed me—at least five times—that he couldn't find a girlfriend due to bad acne.

Then the sexual revolution hit Missoula, arriving with a freight train's force. Not even Wesley House Methodists were immune. Breaking down sexual barriers seemed one more step in my evolution begun in Mr. Dunsmore's class. In my junior year I slept with a boy before I asked his last name.

The novelty of sex soon faded. I quit dating in my senior year. But just as with Cynthia, when I gave up hope I found a best friend, a Great Falls boy, tolerant of earnestness, whom I would marry. I felt an instant bond when Mike revealed that his family had been forced into public housing for three years after his father's death.

*

The cramped bus, its tiny heater chuffing, passed by isolated farms in winter slumber. At last the Missouri River bridge appeared. The twin-arched bridge, spanning rough breaks, looked smaller than in fall, but the towering breaks were the same. Rugged cliffs and spires with gaudy red-orange streaks—sediments baked by lightning-ignited coal seams—were still mysterious, aloof from low hills below.

Around a curve, Culbertson sprouted on the prairie. At the Conoco station bus stop, my father in his overshoes paced in soiled snow on a gray day. Dad smiled at me through the van's window, but behind the smile I saw his worry about the smudged sky readying to drop its load of snow.

The serviceman, still frowning over a cigarette, stayed on the bus, his destination one of the remote towns north of the main highway: Froid, Medicine Lake, Plentywood. His bright blond hair and long face suggested he might even be from tiny Dagmar, settled only by Danes. Were his parents proud or resentful that he'd gone away?

Dad hurried to collect my luggage when I stepped off, agitated by my return or by the weather. We got into the car and drove slowly through long hills of unblemished snow. I realized I had missed the silence here. We turned onto the road that ended in our front yard. I looked up to see Mother, round-eyed in the window. Inside we traded a hug, our very first one.

Indoors was fiercely hot from two coal stoves. I followed Dad to the living room where he opened a conversation on the value of school; he was set on me becoming an elementary teacher like Aunt Mary. I didn't admit to passing over an education course for humanities instead.

Mother entered with a tin of Swedish cookies, her annual Christmas treat. Each year she made them with a cookie press in shapes of Christmas trees, stars, and flowers. She was breaking her rule to bring them out with Christmas still a week away, as if I were a guest. I took just one spritz cookie, butter-rich, as a guest might, and did not beg for more. I felt the same churn of confusion that I had on the trip home. I was glad to be honored as a visitor, grown up. But did that mean I no longer belonged here?

After a few days, college began to wear off. Once more the smell of potatoes simmering on the stove at noon gave me a pleasant ache of hunger, as did the scent of muffins in the overheated oven. I could picture the teaspoon of chokecherry jelly Mother inserted into each, her sly attempt to limit jelly. But like mashed potatoes, jelly wasn't rationed at meals, so I always piled on more.

I felt I belonged nowhere during my sixteen days at home. My disorientation was aggravated by heat. My father's fear of freezing demanded that he burn the coal stoves hot all day, so that the house would not chill too much when the fires got low as we slept. In childhood I would sometimes step outside coatless in late afternoon for relief, or lie on my bedroom linoleum. One winter, two tall candles Mother placed on the piano for decoration bent in a swoon.

Mother had washed the men's corduroy trousers I'd slipped out of in fall, held up by a plastic belt from one of her discarded dresses. She had also cleaned, or made as clean as it could be, the sweatshirt I'd shed, acquired by my grandparents from the town dump. They periodically checked out its treasures, walking through the mazes like store aisles.

I wore the clothes every day for a week before my mother washed them, just like before. For the first time the corduroy trousers didn't hang off me—I'd gained fifteen pounds at school.

Mother didn't mention my weight, nor would she when I packed on ten more pounds by spring break. In our world, thin was suspect: thin cattle in drought years when grass was poor, thin children in unpainted shacks on the Indian reservation twenty miles west. Mother wrote in her diary on December 18: "RA came on bus at 4. She looked good—fatter."

In the evenings, Mother brought out the Scrabble game. She could still beat me, though I was officially better educated than she with a college quarter under my plastic belt.

My parents did not ask about grades. I didn't reveal that I might major in English instead of education.

Mother and Dad went mum when I talked about the professors I admired, who with the help of history and literature suggested that the world was a whole lot larger than I'd ever imagined. I did not mention Mr. Dunsmore's long view on the Christian church.

Dad listened from the couch beside the overheated stove, absent-mindedly flicking his knife. Mother perched upright beside him, or came to stand inside the doorway, interrupting herself at kitchen chores. I spouted ideas on women's rights and the Vietnam War that made her look fearful. I hated myself for that and I relished it too: how could I become part and parcel of the university community if I did not leave this one behind?

I couldn't remember being so bored at home. Winter was always languorous, cows lumbering in energy-saving slow motion, chickens in their unheated house crowding together on roosts. Only mice moved swiftly, hurtling themselves along the walls of outbuildings. One day to fill the time, I hiked half a mile through snow to the pasture where Bud and Goldy were consigned in winter. Dad wouldn't waste hay on horses in winter; they had to forage for grass, and find shelter in prickly Russian olive trees around the upper dam. Once a month or so, Dad sent me up to see them with a bucket of rolled barley.

Bud and Goldy hurried toward me from far off, plunging through coulee drifts. Only in winter were the horses glad for my approach, not eyeing me with suspicion and ready to duck away at the glimpse of a halter rope. Now they jostled each other for grain, and let me thump their thick blankets of hide as they munched. Then I felt another change in me among changes that were coming too fast: I felt sorry for the horses. All winter long they scraped snow for food, and in twenty- or thirty- or forty-below-zero weather had only bare branches to slow the wind.

Never before had I allowed myself more than a second's debate about the horses' winter sufferings. In only three months away, I had lost the ability to block that debate.

On that visit I felt that another debate was over: whether I would come back to live in rural eastern Montana. Like Odysseus, I had wandered far; my six-hundred-mile trip had carried me a greater distance from my roots than I had ever imagined. Unlike Odysseus, I would not find my way home.

Sometimes after supper, Mother and I played duets. Perched on chairs, we worked our way through songs we'd played a hundred times, stumbling in familiar places. Then, in the gray sifting light I felt unchanged. The plink and grumble of what I heard now as a slightly out-of-tune piano still made its way to the midst of me. Time was turned back, and my leaving was undone.

I watched each of my parents separately lift and examine *The Odyssey* paperback book. Then they set it down carefully again, as if they didn't wish to disturb it for fear of releasing an unpleasant odor in the house. Or—more painful to me—they handled it gingerly, like items they lifted on the gift shelf of Culbertson Drug. They could never afford the crystal clocks and little figurines. But my parents did not want them anyway: things only beautiful, and useless.

Return Home

Violets

Thirty years after leaving home, I coast down the long hill into Culbertson on a dull November day. As always, I glimpse more changes in town: fewer stores and churches, even bars. But on my two or three visits a year—from Missoula, Tucson, Seattle, then Great Falls, where I landed fifteen years ago—my parents have stayed the same.

Except this time. I turn north off the highway, and arrive almost immediately at the hospital at town's edge. Then I sit in the lot near a scatter of cars as darkness lowers. I do not go inside because all day long I have carried a picture of my mother in my mind, a picture I do not want replaced. But I know that farther down the road my father is waiting for me, perhaps even holding supper. "It might not be much," he said over the phone, "pork and beans over toast. But hot."

Nurses are huddled in the brilliant light of a central station as I go in. Spokes lead off into several wings of nursing home, and the single wing of hospital—eight rooms. The nurses, smiling, look up as I enter, and I hear one call my name. I glance at them: one tall, one short, a chubby one with light glinting off her glasses. I don't know any of them. "We've been waiting for you," one says. "We knew you were coming." I feel myself soften, though this was the kind of familiarity I was anxious to escape years ago, ending up in a city where still I remain anonymous.

The nurses direct me to a room just off their bay. It is large, darkened, with a single bed in its midst.

I see my mother's hair first, frizzed as always after a perm. Below, her body seems shrunken. She has always been small; now she seems like a child curled along the gleaming rail of her bed.

Mother lies motionless; the nurses have told me the stroke has exhausted her. I begin to make out her features: a slender nose, and a rosebud mouth that at seventy-four can still drop open in surprise. I imagine her look when waking this morning to make Sunday waffles and instead falling over in stroke.

The nurses have warned me that my mother's left side is paralyzed, the paralysis extending upward into her face. Now I am shocked by the face emerging in the dark: sagged, fast-forwarded to old age. As never before, I see how my mother resembles *her* mother—high, Scandinavian cheekbones pressed against translucent skin. "Mother?" I say. Her eyes do not open. I feel relief that she is unconscious, shielded from all that has occurred.

Suddenly, she stirs. Her eyes are tightly closed but I see her mouth begin to work, and at last hear words, soft but distinct: "I hate to have you see me like this."

✳

At home, Dad and I are silent over a plain supper. My father eats quickly, still his habit in retirement; I relax in the slipstream of his vigor that is always an assurance to me.

The telephone rings. It's not the hospital, but my husband in Great Falls; Dad hurriedly hands the phone my way.

After more than two decades, Mike is still a stranger in this house. So is my entire family. Beginning when my kids were small, my parents' faces lit at our arrival, and Mother hurried to sprinkle M&Ms into my children's cupped palms. Then Mother and Dad settled to watch the kids unpack toys and books. All of the books were new; none came from a dump. Mother gaped at my daughter's nine-volume *Little House on the Prairie* boxed set. Dad piped up with ideas for entertainment, always referring to us in third person: "Maybe the company would like to see the north dam."

Mike is cheerful over the phone; he's ordered pizza for the kids. He chatters on about the day's events. Now I wonder if it's not his education or his city upbringing but his durable cheerfulness that is off-putting to Dad.

Once more I feel the strain of habits I haven't entirely left behind. My husband's inquiries, his encouragement, the greetings that he wishes me to pass along interrupt a transaction of silence Dad and I have made. Dad listens to the call, stirring a cup of instant coffee as his face clouds.

✳

The next day Dad and I prepare to visit Mother together. I change my clothes in the cramped spare room, once Ginny's room; her name remains in foil letters on the door.

My parents bought their mobile home fifteen years ago, placing it just a few feet from the house; in a heavy coat Mother had to squeeze between them. The mobile home is no larger but is more modern than the house: electric heat instead of coal, and the bathroom real—not a cramped afterthought carved from a bedroom. Some of their furniture they left in the house: naked spring beds; a couch; my mother's 1940s waterfall dresser, its veneer lifting. But my mother and father bumped the wringer washer across the yard and up the steps into the new bathroom. The house, still sturdy, remains beside the mobile home like a poor relation, an accumulator of outdated clothing and tired appliances.

In fifteen years nothing seems to have changed inside the mobile home, only a creeping dinginess that reminds me of the old house. In this room are cheap gold curtains, sun-faded except in folds where their sheen remains.

When I step outside, my father is waiting. He has backed the car out of its shedlike garage to warm for the drive into town. He stands a little bent beside the car. He is dressed in town wear—Levis and a pearl-snap shirt. In shiny miniature on his belt buckle, a cowboy rides a bronc.

I remember my own cowboy days. I would saddle up stubborn Goldy to jog across the prairie singing "Git Along, Little Dogies," all five verses, memorized from a library book. If the big orange Great Northern Streamliner approached—hurtling daily east and west to Chicago and the coast—I kicked Goldy up a hill above the tracks. There I slouched in the saddle with a bored cowboy look, though I feared at any moment evil Goldy might yank loose the reins and stretch out in a gallop toward home. I tried to glimpse in the tiny faces in the train windows envy of my cowboy life.

A few times a year Dad and I were cowboys together. We wrangled cows, moving them to the north pasture, then back again, and gathering them to brand calves in spring. The cows—which ignored Bud and Goldy grazing at their fringes in the pasture—got white-eyed, and clumsily milled and bawled and banged into each other when the horses came around dressed in creaking and jangling gear. Afterward, we released the horses into the pasture to graze peacefully again beside the cattle.

Our cowboying was a relief from farm chores. It wasn't necessarily cleaner—sweaty horses, manure splatted by anxious cows. A calf suddenly breaking from the herd might have to be forcibly flushed from tick-infested coulee brush. My father's own cowboying had been brief—a stint of breaking neighbors' horses when he bached in a cabin across the river, but he had captured its pleasure: freedom from crop-raising's never-ending worry about weather.

Horses still decorate hills near and far. But now four-wheeled ATVs wait outside farmhouse doors. They don't require catching and saddling before hopping aboard to check fences and move cows. Like horses, all-terrain vehicles scramble up and down rolling hills without complaint. But unlike horses, ATVs won't balk at charging up a hill so steep they might tip. These days, more ATVs than horses kill and cripple riders.

Dad, waiting at the car for our trip to the hospital, doffs his hat as I approach. I cringe to think that even under these circumstances he is practicing his extreme good manners. Despite his reserve, Dad exhibits a kind of flamboyance in manners, in town sweeping off his hat when speaking to women or even meeting them on the street. I have seen women startle at this, then smile in pleasure.

My father, placing his wide-brimmed hat on the seat between us, folds his long legs into the car and drives off, with me in my mother's place beside him.

At the hospital, we tiptoe in to where Mother lies limp. I start a story, trying to fill up the silence; she studies me through slitted eyes as I talk. I describe this morning's Cream of Wheat—forgotten on its back burner as Dad labored to make perfect toast. I exaggerate, but I see that my father doesn't mind. He is standing at my mother's bedside, stiffly, hat in hand, but wearing a little smile as he listens. I end the story declaring that the hardened cereal had to be served in slices. I wait for their laughter.

It doesn't come. I look at Dad, who stands as if at attention beside Mother. Now I see how tightly he grips his hat, crushing its brim. It is his best hat—a gray Resistol—that at home will be tipped back into its box on the closet shelf.

Mother stares at me. Of course, she is only tired; still, her look freezes me. I rake my memory for other times she has given me her penetrating glance; I remember the few times I roused her anger in childhood. My mother seems transfixed. I begin to imagine she's seeing something in me that she hasn't before—as if the stroke has dropped some veil.

A dozen years ago when her breast cancer struck, it was I who arrived on the scene, giving myself over to Mother's recovery. Dwight phoned from California to ask if he should come. "Never mind," I'd said, and then did it all: coming home to clean and cook and receive phone calls, even discouraging my brother from sending flowers. Instead, I bought her flowers in town in the purples and blues I knew she'd enjoy.

A dozen years ago I felt the nurses' admiring eyes as every day I marched into the hospital, my father in tow. Now, though I've encouraged Dwight to send flowers, I yearn to be the one to make Mother well again.

I think she sees through this.

✳

123   VIOLETS

Midday at home I cook a real dinner—meat loaf and squash. I find some of my mother's rolls, and dig around in the refrigerator for chokecherry jelly. It distresses me to the point of nausea to putter about her kitchen, disturbing the clutter that is so much her: a scrubbed tin can, pencils sharpened to stubs, a couple of ancient recipes removed from their box and tucked between canisters. After dinner, with the oven still warm from meat loaf, I decide to make a cake, dessert I can serve to Dad for days. I flip through the tattered recipes in her box. They're all waiting—one-bowl fudge cake, sunshine cake, lazy daisy cake, minute frosting—bringing back the meals of childhood always crowned by cake, one square each.

But in the end I don't make anything. Mother hasn't noted directions for baking, and I don't remember how: baking from scratch was something else I was glad to escape all those years ago.

I tell my father, whose eyes had brightened at the mention of cake, that I don't have all the ingredients. Since my mother's stroke he has seemed largely himself: rushing in and out of the house at chores, even whistling as he cooked—too hot, too long—our cereal in the morning. Now he hesitates, glancing to the counter at my mother's stairstep row of canisters, the largest one still floury from her last bout of baking. At last he shrugs. "We'll buy doughnuts," he says.

Before I do dinner dishes I clean the sink, the drainboard and dish rack, scouring them of a creep of slime that has always on visits home made me cringe. In the afternoon I wash the bath rugs and scrub the toilet and surrounding floor twice. I am unable to remove all the smell—the furry green toilet seat cover retains an odor though it waves in a brisk wind overnight.

All afternoon I work while Dad disappears outside in chores of his own. I scrub walls, cupboard doors flecked with batter, the greasy earmark on the phone. I clean out nests of things—plastic bags opaque with use, crumbling twist ties.

Finally, I pitch out half of the African violets; reducing their clutter is a dream I've had on every visit home. They crowd the coffee table in pots and tin cans, and form an overlapping forest on the spare room's chest of drawers. On this visit I count twenty-eight. I winnow out fourteen plants, some in feeble bloom, and carry them outdoors.

From the front steps I listen for Dad, though he is unlikely to object, never having acknowledged indoor plants. I dig out the rusty nail buried with each—Mother's bargain fertilizer. I loosen the first violet; beneath the plant's dull, dust-laden leaves the roots are thick and intertwining, vigorously resisting removal.

I dig out plant after plant, and with all my strength hurtle them out of sight onto the prairie. Another story for my Dallas-transplant neighbors, I think. My mother and father—who have visited me twice in thirty years—are at least good for colorful stories. I know I'll defend the violets to Dwight, himself visited by our parents just once since he left home. I rehearse our exchange. Dwight will focus on the tortured roots in cramped cans; I'll recall the pale blossoms won by Mother with only junk fertilizer in thin soil.

*

On the third day, Dad and I drive into town in the afternoon. Mother is still shrunken in the hospital bed. But now her eyes are wide open: I see the fear in them.

This time I am silent, and after awhile my mother and father begin to talk. I am lulled by it, small talk about the community in which all their lives have been spent. Together, they flesh out the skeletal report, provided by a nurse, of someone's death. She was married to Axel Antonson, my mother says. She was born a Jensen, my father provides—a fact, though the maiden name of the eighty-year-old woman seems to me unimaginably deep in the past.

Suddenly Mother, turning to me, sticks out her tongue.

For the second time in as many days, I feel a stab that she is angry at me. I have sat quietly as they talked, but perhaps she has seen my attention wander. I have been studying the get-well cards on her board, their bland pastel hues.

"Look," my mother insists, and then I see it. Her tongue is disfigured; pale, mottled, as if a thick, whitish net has been cast over it.

"They had me sip hot broth," Mother says. She is matter-of-fact. "I didn't feel it happen."

My mother's body, though shrunken, is unblemished by stroke. I stare at her tongue; the skin is white, coagulated. I feel myself sink—

lower even than when listening to my father stammer over the phone that Mother had had a stroke and might not live.

Driving home, my father announces that it is time to empty the rain barrel. I look over at him. Though the fall chore must be done, the day is late, midafternoon. I see that Dad is driving sixty, fast for him, his body leaned forward over the wheel. Yesterday he began to lengthen the snow fence bordering the west edge of our farm, pounding metal posts into the prairie. "It's going to be a big snow year," he said.

The rain barrel, silvery galvanized steel, sits as always beneath the eaves. During summers of my childhood it was cool, welcoming, an oasis in the heat. Even in late summer, when the water was low and brackish, I would duck my head inside to feel I had entered another world. Strange bugs lived there: not the dull, dusty ones of our crops and garden, but ones that glittered at me; coppery, sleek.

My father, already dipping a bucket, pauses to say that leaving the water to freeze over winter will make the barrel burst. I look around for a bucket, ready to fit into the groove of farm work again. But Dad has brought only one.

I lean into the barrel where ice is forming. I tug out a piece as big as a banquet platter. "Look," I call to my father as he swings past, bucket streaming. Always, outdoor work absorbs him; I wait for a nod or gruff reply.

Dad halts, staring at me and at the ice. Finally, he says: "Very picturesque."

He turns away; the words echo in my mind. Each word was spoken carefully, its syllables distinct. I think of Dad in town lifting his hat to people he meets on the street, some of them strangers.

I haven't done chores since I left home, but I thought that role still waited for me. I watch my father tramp by, lost in the rhythm of dipping a bucket into the barrel and striding to hurl the water out. I yearn to join him, to wake tomorrow with a callous on my palm from the wire handle. But even without my own family, I am "company" here.

*

On the fourth day of my visit, we bring Mother news. She seems dull as we enter, but as we talk her face begins to light.

The church had phoned asking for contributions to their rummage sale, mentioning last year's African violets. Dad and I had delivered three plants, two in bloom, on our trip to the hospital. The minister's wife pounced on them the minute they hit the table.

"She bought mine last year," Mother says, looking pleased. I'm beginning to hear her slurred voice as normal.

"I wonder if the violets will remember each other," I joke.

Mother studies something across the room. "I wonder."

That evening, seated beside my father on the couch, I listen to the kitchen clock's tick, and remember Mother's busyness even at night. There would be sounds of tidying up—the clamor of pans nestled back in their cupboard, the ring of silverware tossed into its drawer. Sometimes the whir of the mixer announced a replenishment to her supply of cakes. The measuring spoons' high clatter, the groan of the oven door, carried across to Dad and me on the couch; Dad glanced to follow Mother's progress.

There's nothing large about my parents' mobile home, but suddenly the undivided living room and kitchen where we sit seems cavernous. I look down at the coffee table, almost bare, its clutter removed, as are three more African violets.

Beside me, Dad stirs and clears his throat. "It's 8:30," he says. Then, as in all the days of my memory, he rises and disappears to bed.

✳

On the fifth day, I wash clothes. I sort through my mother's closet, pulling slacks and their colorful tops off hangers. I check each one, but in the end decide to wash them all. Slipping the fresh-smelling clothes, dried in the wind, back onto the shoulders of hangers, I search for loosened buttons, torn seams. I fix them all. I decide to replace the elastic in the waistband of a pair of navy slacks. I pull out the old elastic, crumpled and ugly, and replace it with new that I find in Mother's drawer. When I am finished I tug at the waist, which snaps satisfyingly.

In the afternoon we drive to the hospital. Entering my mother's room, I scan as always for symptoms of recovery. Her bed seems closer to the window, by a foot or so—I hurry over. Has she suddenly asked to see outside? She is still in a gown, but I see that her salt-and-pepper curls have been rearranged; someone has tried to tame them.

But Mother lies limp in her bed. The sun dazzles into the room, inviting. The entire floor gleams; I see its fresh wax coat. I picture the bed shifted during cleaning, someone failing to move it back.

Mother turns on us a smile that has an abstracted air; each time we enter I feel we force her from some deep, all-absorbing new world. The left side of her face still seems deflated, as does her left arm and curled fingers. I think of the urgency with which I repaired her clothes. I had even aligned them perfectly in the closet: short-sleeved with short-sleeved, long with long. Passing by, I peeked inside just to admire them.

My father and I don't speak. We stand beside the bed, looking down at Mother.

But on the drive home Dad, clearing his throat, says suddenly: "She's just a ghost of herself."

I turn away and look outside the window. Prairie grass and fields of straw are shimmery under the sun. I can't reply, as if Mother's stroke has paralyzed me too.

I think how Dad is a ghost himself, of the father he scorned. Not just in his formal diction, but in his habit of memorizing poetic Bible verse. "The Lord tempers the wind to the shorn lamb," my grandfather wrote as the drought of the 'teens began. He later amended: "Those lambs are in trouble."

Like the father before him, Dad has strained relations with his son. Dwight defines Dad as a tyrant.

Now I bend a little Dwight's way. I think of my alternate life in Great Falls, where the kids will eat pizza again, foreign to my parents, as are milkshakes, tacos, Chinese food, lasagna. I wish that my old and new lives would overlap, easing visits home. During the day-long drive to my parents' home, I nag Dell and Andy: don't waste food—no Cheerios left floating in milk; don't waste cistern water.

At meals here, my children stare at canned vegetables—and eat bites at my reproachful look. I talk them out of showering, urging them to bathe in just a few inches of water in the tub.

Tonight, Dad is silent across from me at the crowded supper table.

Between us are loaves of bread, cans of fruit and soup and stew. Each day he unloads groceries onto the table, carrying none to cupboard shelves. Arriving here, I was repelled by the clutter, but lately it's seemed right. Like the mess involved in camping, it holds a cheerful promise: this is temporary.

Then Dad tips forward across two mounds of bread, twin haystacks on the cluttered field of table, and says: "When I promised your mother forty years, it seemed like an eternity."

I shrink in my chair. At meals, our best time together, I want to put the pending loss aside.

Maybe I can't. I have been digging around in a jar of crabapple pickles, a single one I was glad to find on the cellar shelf. Every year Mother makes crabapple pickles, plucking the fruit from high in their aging trees, boiling the tiny apples whole in syrup. She makes pickles of cucumbers and beets, even the rind of watermelon. But crabapple ones are my favorite, sweet and spicy with a sour kick. I cradle them in my fingertips, carefully nibbling at the tiny core.

With my fork I chase an apple, aswirl in its cinnamon-flecked syrup, around the jar. I trap the pickle, large and plump, that has evaded me.

Wet years or drought, I've always known there will be gleaming dark jars of pickles on the cellar shelf.

Then I press the trapped pickle in the jar against the glass—and see it's the last one.

*

On the sixth day, we learn that Mother will need rehabilitation. For several months, the doctor says. He talks of therapy, recovery, functions restored, though I think his face looks doubtful as he speaks.

Then we discover how far we are from specialized care. The nearest rehabilitation center, deep in Dakota, is two hundred miles away, too far for my father to manage regular visits. The doctor suggests a hospital in my city. It's impossibly far from my father of course, but at least I could visit her every day.

But we can't get her there. The train doesn't stop at Great Falls anymore, nor does a connecting branch still exist. Flying takes most of the day, a circuitous route involving a layover. Finally, Dad engages a man who—not without expense—will fly her four hundred miles in less than two hours.

I think of a story Mother used to tell. During her childhood, before the thirties' drought emptied the country out, she used to dash across the prairie after the train. The little local stopped at every settlement, no matter how tiny; it could even be flagged down.

The man with the plane, from a neighboring town, is unknown to us; he bears the racy name of Reno McKay. I think of the possibility ahead of years of nursing homes, galling my mother and depleting my father's savings, and guiltily imagine Reno McKay making a careless move and all of my mother's problems dissolving instantly in a fiery crash.

In the hospital room, we tell Mother the plan. She looks apprehensive as I knew she would, though she has flown once before, to visit her parents at Aunt Claire's home in California. She says: "Maybe the plane will crash and this will be over at once."

That evening, alone in the house, I begin to pack my mother for her journey. Back in the silent bedroom, I sift through aging socks and underwear in her drawer for dress-up ones. I feel myself on alert as I go through things—as if I'm a kid again, on the prowl for secrets in my parents' bedroom.

The top of the dresser is cluttered with stuff—lipsticks and rouge I've glimpsed since my childhood, metal cases burnished by age. Packed together on a tray are little perfumes, gifts from my father, I think. I try to recall a scent I associate with Mother. Then before I can think, I lift a bottle and squirt some on myself; a cloud drifts down on my forearm. The scent is strong.

I hear the door slam, my father whistling to himself as he often does when cheered by work outdoors. Suddenly I panic. I smell myself strongly, a lilac fragrance that I am beginning to recall on Mother. I remember sitting beside her in church, everything hushed, Mother looking up at the minister expectantly.

I rush out of the bedroom and into the bathroom, where I soap my forearm vigorously, twice. I rinse and sniff: the smell remains. Lined up, newly neatened by me, are rows of my father's aftershave, green and icy blue in their containers. Enough to drown my mother's scent—but then how to get rid of that?

I hear rustles on the couch, Dad rereading the newspaper. I leave the bathroom and head down the hall to the kitchen where I manage to avoid my father. I neaten dishes on their shelves and polish Mother's canisters until they gleam. I turn my back to Dad at 8:30 on the dot, when he rises and brushes past to bed.

*

On the seventh day, at the end of my visit, there is a change. Mother is sitting upright as we enter her room, her bed cranked forward. Sitting up! I feel heartened by its normalcy. The curtains are open and the sun blazes in. The kind sun—all week long it has shone, tempering sharp fall days.

Mother doesn't turn her head as we enter. I cross the room and then stop short at what I see. She is wearing only a hospital gown, bedcovers pushed off into a crumple. Her right leg, the good one, is drawn up, and the gown has fallen open to her thigh.

I stare at the milky thigh that I'm not sure I have seen before.

For years Mother wore housedresses every day. She ordered them from catalogues, expert at flipping to them at the end of women's wear where fashion dwindled. The dresses seemed all alike, plain-cut in cheery prints. Finally, yielding to fashion, she made the switch to slacks. They too seemed alike, synthetic knit in friendly shades of brown and blue.

Now my mother, at ease, lounges like a teenager on a beach. I look outside where frost still clings to the grass in shadows. Mother, glancing at us long enough to smile, shifts her leg but it doesn't lower.

My father, standing, is staring at her. He is kneading the brim of his hat with his fingertips. Finally, he asks, "Aren't you cold?"

That afternoon Dad and I sit as always on the couch together during a pause from chores. Across from us the late day's sun slants in; the curtains glow.

I cast around for a way to begin conversation; it's my last day here. I think about the weather, mild still despite my father's warning of a hard year.

Dad wears his grimy work overalls in whose pocket he has discovered his knife. He flicks the blade open-shut, open-shut, gazing out the window. I think this is the first he's fiddled with his knife since my arrival, and I decide to take it as a sign of normalcy. He'll be okay without Mother.

Then he says suddenly: "Why did they haul her all the way to Williston for an x-ray?"

For a minute, I can't think. I stare at the curtains' bulbous glow.

I remember it was my father himself who told me about the tests performed across the Dakota line. Mother had gone by ambulance there the same day of her stroke. Later the doctor had stopped in the hospital hallway to tell us why.

"Remember," I say, "she got a brain scan there. The doctor said it showed a stroke. On the right side of her head."

Dad hesitates, then turns on me a disgusted look. "Must be the doctor in town can't do that."

"It's a brain scan," I reply. I hear my voice louder. "The hospital in town hasn't got the right equipment."

I look at my father, whose face is set. He has halted his knife. I wait for my words to sink in while the last of the sun tips the leaves of the African violets before us.

"That basement is full of machines!" Dad erupts. "Must be no one knows how to use them!"

The shock of his outburst propels me toward a realization I've been ducking since I arrived: despite my father's health and strength—at eighty-four he walks briskly, and still spades up a large garden—he will *not* endure well my mother's illness.

All their married lives, my parents rehearsed to survive the wrong tragedy: that of want. They can hold their own with anyone if poverty arrives; I picture them boiling up shoe leather. But in their retreat from the world they have not prepared to lose each other.

I think of how my life differs from theirs: meals, vacation trips, music lessons for the kids, an actual turkey at Thanksgiving (Mother bought, even on our visits, cheap turkey rolls—bits of dark and white meat pressed into a log shape). Now I wonder if the chasm between us is not just the choices I've made—money down the drain for nonessentials, emotions freely spent (when Mike hugged the kids goodnight, Mother and Dad ducked their heads in embarrassment), but that in contrast to them, clones of their own parents, I've dared to make choices at all.

In the the mobile home, I sit motionless, inhaling a stale scent singularly my parents' that none of my efforts has washed out. Suddenly Dad rises and crosses the room for his chore coat, since Mother's illness draped onto chairs instead of its closet hook, and disappears outside.

I settle on leftovers for supper. After washing dishes, I am glad for the excuse to hole up in the spare room, packing for my departure. From the couch, I hear a rustle of newspapers. After a while the TV blasts on, clicks through its three channels, and is off again.

I hear Dad begin to hum, something plucked from the scores of old dance tunes my mother and he together committed to memory.

Though I am packed, I stall going out into the living room.

Then I hear nothing from down the hall; my father, I am certain, is asleep. I am grateful for his sleep, blurring the edges of the day. He will wake after dark, feeling his way down the hallway to bed in half-stupor.

I switch off my light and lie looking out the window as darkness gathers. I listen for the wind, always rising at night, in childhood frightening me from sleep with its fury. Tonight the wind is absent.

Then I hear Dad clear his throat; he hasn't been asleep after all.

"8:30," he says, his voice ringing out, and passes down the long hallway to bed.

*

My last morning, I rise to the smell of pancakes. I dress and stumble into the kitchen to see they are a limp version of Mother's—collapsed across each other on the plate—but my father seems pleased. He shoves them toward me as I settle myself at the table. "Eat up for your trip," he says.

He seems himself this morning, and I realize this is something he enjoys—the complication of sending me on my way. There are problems to solve: have I forgotten anything? What can I take for a lunch?

I imagine that he has already eyed my car's tires and checked its fluids.

I eat as many pancakes as I can manage. I try to carry dishes to the sink but Dad objects. "I've got all day for that," he says.

The car is loaded at last and I seat myself inside. Dad watches from the front steps. This morning he wears a good shirt, a neat blue check with shiny snaps.

I start the car, lifting my hand for a last wave, when I notice that his Levis are unzipped.

This morning he'll drive to town to visit Mother. I know where he will park. Entering the hospital, he will lift his hat to the nurses, who will smile in return.

But this time I imagine them hesitating, their gaze lingering. Perhaps they will notice, too, his shave this morning is not so smooth, several missed patches on his cheeks looking like little scrub plants. Despite my father's height, his cowboy look and courtly air, something will change for them; I see their smiles dim.

My father stands tall on the steps, the wind blowing around him. Behind him, the last of my mother's towels I've washed are waving on the line. The wind rattles something near his feet. A broken piece of flowerpot, just trash now. I think of the African violets scattered as far as I can throw. Now I wish I'd carried them into town instead, crowding them onto Mother's windowsill.

But the windowsill is tiny. She ignores the flowers that fill it, sent by Dwight.

I look up from my musing to see Dad's eyes still on me. Suddenly, I am in a rush to get back home. I release the gear and the car drifts backward down the drive; I wave and pull away.

Journey

"Oh dear, poor Hazel," my mother says from her hospital bed.

She isn't referring to herself, a sister, or even a maiden aunt, but her silly cat. Hazel's a white, fluffy, unfarmlike cat who twines around my mother's feet as she steps outside, following her from sheds to barn to garden and home again. Hazel disappears on my visits, including this one; I get glimpses of her like a ghost.

I've come to help Dad arrange for Mother's rehabilitation, aided by Dwight in California over the phone. We think we've got it nailed down; plans are finalized for flying Mother to Great Falls. Even the weather is cooperating—eastern Montana is not yet a below-zero icebox, though it's November.

I tell Mother that Hazel's fine, though my views of her are distant. Hazel balances on the porch rail of their mobile home, beaming messages in to send my mother out, scattering whenever my father and I appear.

Dad is silent beside Mother's bed. It's almost her last day here, and I know they've hardly been apart before. "I guess you're in charge of Hazel," I say. It's a joke; my father is not one for pets. Still I secretly hope that in my mother's absence he can connect with the cat.

He doesn't seem to hear.

A nurse pops in, followed by an aide and then another. In the tiny hospital they've come to tell my mother good-bye.

Mother, petite, sits propped in bed. She wears a touch of lipstick and her squarish blue-framed glasses, lending an air of rapt attention to the nurses' tales of recovery from stroke:

"Chandler Stolz was back on his feet in a month. Now he's turning out windmills in his woodshop again."

"Marian Olson has to use a cane but gets around."

Politely, no one mentions Chris Hansen, a farmer once like my father, who's out of earshot in another wing where he permanently resides. "Helpme-helpme-helpme-helpme," he calls all day to no one.

I tell Mother I'll see her soon. It's been so many years since we've really visited that I think of her upcoming stay in Great Falls as a long sleepover—her bed only ten blocks away from mine.

Mother is pleased at the thought of seeing my kids again. She reminds Dad to keep busy around the farm.

The next day, I drive the all-day trip home ahead of her. I clean up the house when I get there, as I did for their single "drive-by" visit to Great Falls—even in retirement, with no cows and chickens, they couldn't leave the farm for more than three days.

Right after her stroke, Mother had asked me to keep up her diary, and waiting for her I fill in the entire week at once, feeling guilty. I think she imagines herself one day reading it as I've seen her browse back through other diaries—forming an unbroken record begun when she was a teenager.

When she arrives in Great Falls, I miss her little plane at the airport. I drive straight to the hospital, where I find her in the rehabilitation unit just being put into bed.

She is so happy to see me! We clasp hands—right hands; her left hand is limp—and I sit beside her helping the nurse take a history. I enjoy it; Mother remembers most things, and I'm able to fill in the rest. I'm proud of my mother, proud to hear her say she's never smoked, and I chuckle as she vehemently declares she's never been a drinker. She's an innocent: all her days spent in a few square miles in the emptiest corner of our empty state.

In a fresh gown and with an unwrinkled pillow beneath her head, my mother looks good. Improved, I think, though I've perched myself to view her right side. Beneath the sheet, I see her left arm ending in its useless curl.

Mother is sleepy, one of the effects of stroke that the doctor seems sure will vanish. I say good-bye, promising to return this evening to phone Dad, and especially her sister.

This year stroke's a family affair. Three months ago in California, Aunt Claire was struck down, also her left side paralyzed. Though Claire is eighty-two and my mother seventy-four, on the phone to each other they seem astonished at what has occurred. "The girls," my grandmother always called them.

Aunt Claire, bold as my mother is meek, had seemed her red-haired, feisty self over the phone, though her words were slowed to a drawl. "Isn't this the limit?" she'd said.

When I return to the hospital in the evening I climb the stairs slowly, four flights. In her room Mother is asleep, so soundly I do not try to wake her. I settle in a chair beside her bed and realize that she at last seems familiar to me: her new lopsided self, left side in retreat.

I sit a long time before I remember just how she looked before.

The next day Mother begins a schedule of therapies. There is occupational therapy—teaching her to dress an uncooperative left side—and physical therapy. Speech therapy will first teach her to read with the loss of left-side peripheral vision.

The speech therapist starts with a menu, and Mother seems pleased: eating out in the town café is her favorite indulgence. "Salad sand-wich," she reads slowly, then follows the dotted line to the price: "Sixty cents."

She frowns at the menu, studying it. I see her mouth the words again. She lowers the menu and gives me the imploring look that since her stroke has made me rush to help her. This time I think I shouldn't; I see hurt spring in her eyes.

Then the therapist leans and taps the left edge of the menu with his pencil—as day after day, week after week I will see him do—until at last Mother sees the word she missed.

"*Egg* salad sandwich—oh, for heaven's sake," she says.

Later the therapist tells me that vision damage in stroke is tricky, involving the brain. "Forget it," her brain says all day long: "Nothing there on the left anymore; don't even bother to check."

In the first week Mother manages some success: on two separate days she is continent. The nurses greet me with the news at my arrival.

One day I see that we aren't the only family pair in rehabilitation. Wheeling down the hall to therapy, we meet a second mother-daughter duo, the mother also wheelchair-bound, left arm limp.

For a few days I avoid contact. Both the mother and daughter are nicely dressed. I've supplemented my mother's wardrobe out of my own pocket with a few colorful sweatshirts, but this woman and her daughter are leagues ahead of us. The daughter is jewel-bedecked. The mother appears to have her hair regularly styled, and even the nails of her useless hand gleam with polish.

Then one day as we maneuver past I hear the mother speak— sounding like my mother, as if her left jaw is packed with gravel—and I look up at the daughter; our eyes meet. She smiles. Then we smile whenever we see each other, making me feel, as I hope it does my mother too, that we're all part of a team pulling together.

One morning as I enter her room, Mother announces that mice have visited. She awoke at dawn, she said—she and Dad were always early risers—and saw their droppings on the bedside tray.

I look at the shiny clean tray and feel my heart sink. My scrupulous mother—I cannot remember in all my life doubting her word before.

"Oh, Mother," I say, "I wouldn't think so. Not in a nice hospital like this."

She shakes her head. "I wouldn't think so, either."

Mother's not afraid of mice, having peeled them daily from traps in the granary and sheds to toss at the cat. She was not alarmed when mice occasionally invaded her home.

I know that she longs for home. She pores over the slender pages of the weekly hometown paper sent by Dad. I read out loud news in the left-hand columns that she misses.

I decide we'll call Dad every day. Our calls are brief, my father always hesitant over the phone. He struggles to fill in the silences with bits of news.

One day he mentions the cat. He begins to take an interest in what she eats, though even Mother would fling only leftovers—slimy baloney, ancient American cheese—into the margarine tub outside the door as supplement to her foraged diet.

Dad becomes obsessed with feeding the cat, every day reporting success or failure. She will eat leftover Cream of Wheat. She hates jelly doughnuts. He fumes when she turns up her nose at milk he's heated in a saucepan on the stove.

Jelly doughnuts! Mother sighs, handing the phone my way with the same look of resignation she greets shots, enemas, therapies, tests.

At the evening meal, the dressed-up daughter's mother and mine are assigned a table together. The daughter and I begin to talk. We swap stroke dates—her mother was stricken just a couple of days after mine. We watch our mothers eat, helping a little. The other mother does better, her fork even roaming by itself to the left edge of the tray. Then the daughter glances at me and we smile.

I try to encourage Mother to talk; instead, she turns to me: "Tell them about Hazel." I describe my mother's cat, its acrobatics—clinging to the shed roof outside the kitchen window to glower at my parents during meals. I tell about the hiding places in outbuildings that Hazel likes to spring from in surprise. Everyone smiles at the stories.

One day I arrive late. I had let down a little at home and was slow in getting going my own family's meal. But while hurrying to the hospital, I decide my delay may be a good thing. I picture my mother sitting with the two at our table, congenial. I imagine, without my prodding, Mother taking up her fork on her own. Without my encouragement, digging into tonight's version of hospital food and putting some meat on her bones—she's slipped below one hundred pounds.

When I step into the dining room I see Mother at once, slumped, asleep over her tray. A jewel of spit has formed at her mouth—her drool something else I've gotten used to, though I notice that many of the other patients aren't similarly afflicted.

Mother's face is inches from her meal: peas in gelid butter sauce; a macaroni-and-cheese dish, untouched, its orange surface dulled. I

look across at the other woman and daughter, like everyone else waiting for their emptied tray's removal. They are staring at my mother.

When I glance at them, they look away.

*

Several times a week I bring my children to visit; never has my
mother seen so much of them, and I hope their presence can inject
her with health and youth.

But the kids are tongue-tied toward their grandmother, and she
is shy with them. I think that some of the clumsy relationship is my
fault.

On every visit home I've been hyper-aware of my kids on my old
turf, pounding the same ground in play, pumping on the same creaky
and probably dangerous tall-poled swing. I've encouraged their rough
play, wanting Mother to think they aren't soft city kids. Then something has happened, like my daughter falling from the top corral
pole she was attempting to twirl around as if it was the jungle gym at
school. She got a few scrapes, and tore a hole in the knee of her new
pink fleece pants.

Dell wasn't concerned, but Mother was: "I hope they don't ruin their
good clothes." Mother's comment rang with worry. In trying hard to
make Mother think the kids were tough, I'd alarmed her instead by
letting them run wild in good clothes. In my childhood, clothes not
stained or worn or fitting badly were strictly reserved for school.

Mother is gentle with my children; I think she loves them. But I
have craved something more. I have wanted her to accept my children
as some kind of prize to her. I have wanted her to feel—as the six of
us filled a pew in the Methodist Church, or one booth for a hot meal
in the Wild West Diner—townspeople's lingering stares. Some of the
same people stared at Rosemary and Ginny, and at our shabby family. My parents still look slightly shabby. But nestled between them
are well-dressed, shiny-haired children. I pack the kids' best clothes
before our trips and lecture them on manners so that they will appear
exceptional.

I have wanted to offer my children up to Mother as expiation for two damaged daughters. And though she is proud of my kids, I don't think she's bought into the idea of swapping out my sisters' pasts.

*

One week I decide to accompany Mother to physical therapy every day. She's nearing the halfway point—two months being her limit here—and I hope to cheer her on.

The therapist is very young. I was with Mother on her first day here when she discovered that he was another Scandinavian, a Jensen. Again today, she pumps him about other Jensens he might know, particularly on the other side of the state.

"No," the therapist says. He smiles.

"Nope.

"No relation."

My mother gives up.

But the therapist doesn't give up on her. Today she'll stand alone, he says.

Mother gives me a fearful look; I try to beam some confidence her way.

The therapist locks her wheelchair, then leans to strap the webbed gate belt around her waist. On his command she will drape her arm around his neck as he pulls.

All day Mother is lifted. From bed to chair, from chair to toilet and at night again to bed, flinging her arm around the necks of strangers to assist each move. At first I had seen Mother hesitate; like my dad, she's not a toucher. I didn't get hugs in childhood, though now on each of my two or three visits home a year we embrace. I calculate, as the therapist finishes cinching the belt, that in her twice-daily work-outs here my mother may have given him more hugs than she has ever given me.

"Now," the therapist says. Mother lifts her good arm to his neck and doesn't take her eyes off me as she struggles to her feet.

I smile and try to force my face into a look of surprise at her success, though the therapist's hand still firmly grips her belt.

"Okay," the therapist says, and he lets go of the belt as Mother gives me a helpless look. She's dressed in a sweatshirt I gave her—a winsome cat on front—and her nicest navy slacks that just a month ago she'd slip on in a minute if my father took a notion to drive into town.

Mother begins to totter. My face aches from smiling. Finally, she collapses into her chair as the therapist grips her belt. "We'll try again tomorrow," he says. He reminds my mother of the catch in her hip that she reported on her history; the hometown doc had labeled it arthritis.

"It might be acting up," the therapist says. "They've ordered x-rays."

Mother sighs.

I go home drained. I'm in bed as early as my two children, but then wake in the middle of the night. I'm angry. I've had a dream, I think, and wait for the dregs of emotion to pass.

But the feeling won't go away. In the silence, the stillness of the night, I realize that this anger has been circling me for a month, beaten back with exhausting efforts toward my mother and with my relentless good cheer.

A memory springs full-blown into my mind: words in a letter written to me about a year ago. In the letter Mother described a visit to her doctor, just routine, to be resupplied with pills for her blood pressure. The doctor had urged on her something new. Years of high blood pressure had increased her risk for stroke, he said, but now an anticoagulant drug could discourage the dangerous clots from forming. Coumadin, the doctor called it; a bit priccy, he said.

I told him no, Mother said in her letter; I told him I felt fine.

Now in the dark I imagine her calculating, on the drive home from town, how many dollars she would save.

I know that our farm has never prospered, the price of wheat always down in the cellar, too many dry years. I know that growing up in the Great Depression left its scars. But in bed in the dark I can't forget the Coumadin, and feel myself led down a black tunnel to other memories.

For just a few more dollars here and there, I could have dressed like the others in school. Always I wore cheap things—sweaters that fuzzed after a single washing, shoes whose leather was fake. The list unfurls in my mind: home haircuts, marking us children at school.

Hot dogs and baloney at meals, our grazing cattle making steaks for someone else.

Saving, saving a penny.

For hours I lie awake in the dark; I can't forgive my mother. I fear that my efforts toward her from now on will be only motion, feelings drained.

The next day I stall my visit until evening. When I enter the room she reaches toward me as if she is drowning.

"They saw a shadow on my x-ray."

✳

Two days later I sit by her bed waiting to hear the results of tests.

Cancer had slipped my mind, as I think it had Mother's too. When news of the stroke reached me I thought: so she won't have to struggle with cancer after all, as if one serious illness obliterated another.

A dozen years had passed since her last cancer bout, taking with it her left breast. Ten years before that, the right. A couple of times since her stroke I'd helped her undress. She'd had the old-fashioned radical mastectomies—all of the breast removed plus chest muscles thrown in for good measure. She looked like an inverted bird, her chest concave.

In her room, I fill up the time by reading aloud her latest get-well cards. Mother has said she's read them all but lifts her eyebrows in surprise at some of the left-side news.

I fasten the cards to her board, straightening yesterday's cards tacked by a nurse. I turn to receive my mother's smile but she is gazing off across the room looking somber. Trying to think of something that will lift her, I remember the cat. My mother has decided to take Dad's ministrations toward the cat in stride. "At least she won't actually starve," Mother says.

"Maybe Hazel is right now setting into a jelly doughnut," I say. My mother's explanation for the cat's name is that she took the fellow who delivered the kitten to her seriously when he said, "Name it after my wife."

Mother turns to me and laughs. I realize I have become fond of her new half-smile and languid laugh.

Then a nurse peeks in to say the oncologist is coming.

The oncologist is short and dark, definitely not Scandinavian. He seems in a hurry, and doesn't meet our eyes as he speaks. "We have three areas to treat," he says. "Left knee, right hip and shoulder."

He adds, "And we'll give you some tamoxifen to discourage anything else. Any questions?"

My mother raises her eyebrows at me, and I try to give her a look of encouragement: just three areas!

✳

The next day we cross town to meet with another oncologist, the expert in radiation. He's different from the first, a real talker. He chats with us in his tiny office that seems to hang off the room where all the action is—it looks as huge as a meat locker when the heavy doors occasionally open.

He chats on and on encouragingly. Radiation shouldn't take too long. It won't hurt, although she'll get some salve for burns. He twirls in his chair to describe the technician who'll deliver the treatments; a Vietnam vet, the doctor says. He lowers his voice to warn, mock-serious, not to inquire about the location of his war wound, a delicate site. I hear Mother's slow-speed chuckle.

At last he turns to the x-rays spread along a high, back-lit screen across the wall. They look like giant versions of the black-and-white negatives familiar to me from childhood: reverse images of pictures Mother snapped of us in clean clothes following baths.

I study the outlines of Mother's bones and am surprised how much they look like the bones I have seen all along in books: the lanky femur, the arm bones' graceful knotting at the elbow. I see three dark streaks of tumors, though the pictures are marred with smudges, making some of them unclear, like negatives from Mother's camera when she took pictures months apart with a dusty lens.

The doctor touches a long streak on a hip bone. "We'll treat here," he says, and then his pointer skips to the spots on a knee and shoulder, "these three. Maybe we'll touch the one on the clavicle."

I look up to see his pointer on one of the smudges I had imagined to be an error on the film.

"Maybe more," the doctor says.

I clearly see, as I think my mother, nodding in exhaustion in her wheelchair, does not, smudges here and here and here . . .

✴

A month later we're headed to Culbertson. I drop by the hospital early to pack Mother and visit. Though the radiation has exhausted her, she has skipped her morning nap.

The sun streams in her window, a nice day for January. It's been a mild winter overall.

I ask her if she's ready to return home—to the hospital at home— and she says: "I'm ready to fly the plane myself."

Dad has engaged the same man to fly her; this time I'll accompany her. We leave soon.

"He's not Scandinavian," Mother says. I have been worried about the pilot, too, envisioning an off-season crop sprayer dodging us under power lines across the state.

But everything goes smoothly. We ride in a handicap van to the airport, where Mike has slipped from work to lift Mother from wheelchair to stretcher. The pilot, friendly, guides the stretcher into the tiny plane through the cargo door, and I settle beside Mother in the single rear seat. As the engine winds she reaches for my hand—she is afraid of flying—and I grip it as we rise into perfectly clear blue sky.

Mother's hand stays tight on mine as the plane glides out. I glance down at her and smile, then turn to lean against the window and look down.

The plane flies north, following swollen hills along the Missouri River, then finally turning east over smooth prairie. I glimpse a lonely farm. I think I should turn back to Mother, but I'm hungry for the scene below: a thumbprint-sized stock pond shines like a quarter tossed onto prairie grass. The farmstead beside it looks clean from this height, nothing shabby or depressing, its discard pile a blur.

This, I think, is what my family fought for: their own manor carved from wilderness. How hard my grandparents struggled for something the size of small change from the air!

I wonder if Grandfather Alexander's elaborate dikes and dams, the hundred diamond willow seedlings he planted along a dammed coulee, would have been visible from this height. He finally left Surprise Ranch after forty years, persuaded to join Grandmother, who'd retired from teaching to a house in town. Ten years later when our family visited the farm, it was invisible even at ground level.

The new owner had demolished the house, and hauled the chicken house and barn to his own place. The land was empty, though somewhere beneath our feet seven horses lay dissolving, perhaps lending themselves to an adjacent robust field of wheat.

"Montana is the land of beginning," Grandfather wrote in 1913 at his decision to homestead. He longed to be part of history here. But history erased him.

Where did my family shelve their disappointment at how stubbornly this land resisted their endeavors? We were teased with good crops now and then, and some did not hail out.

Perhaps my family loved the country itself, its tall tarp of sky that through dry air was blue all the way to the horizon.

Maybe my parents and grandparents stayed because they did not know better. Dwight and I did. Our journey from here may have been launched by TV, transmitted when I was ten from a tower on a hill near Williston. Every day at four o'clock our gunmetal gray set came to life, bringing our rapt family images of a world cleaner and better than our own. Even cowboys dashing over desert plains were scrubbed, and some rode palominos.

Or perhaps television alone didn't change us. Twice removed from our grandparents' zeal, my generation saw with clear eyes how hard this life was on humans, livestock, and wheat. None of my twenty-two classmates is a farmer.

Ninety minutes later, we circle the cracked asphalt airstrip of my hometown. Last year's weeds, blonde in winter, loom into view. No one's around as we land, just my father, who despite his age hurries to greet us.

The handicap van from the hospital, a stone's throw away, arrives; a girl rolls a wheelchair out. I'm disappointed; I had imagined a team of people meeting us. I panic a little; I don't know who will lift my mother from stretcher to chair. The pilot has apologized before the flight; he's recovering from back surgery. My father hurries over. I wave him away.

I can do this, I know. My mother weighs eighty-five pounds, the same as my blond, muscular ten-year-old son whom I last week picked up and hurled onto the couch while wrestling with him.

I lean and place my arms beneath my mother. When I lift she feels so much lighter than my son.

As I gentle her into the wheelchair, I look down and see her eyes flick to me and to the blue bowl of sky in deep and perfect recognition: the sky being examined for weather; her look at me containing all our years.

Then I think I can't stand it. My mother is diapered; her chest is carved away. Tumors are eating her bones, and her left side is numb. She can't even see off the left in each eye, as if wearing a wacky pair of blinders.

But she sees.

✳

Over the months, I travel back and forth across the state between my home and the hospital. Two weeks here, a week there—most mornings I awake not knowing where I am.

When visiting my father, I still get only flashes of Hazel, who wears a perpetually startled look. On the snow-packed steps, I tread carefully around my father's daily offerings: white bread, a doughnut that for weeks seems bakery-fresh thanks to winter weather, a single waffle with a glaze of syrup.

Mother has been told of her condition. But in the mildest way. On the phone to me the doctor says people can live for years with cancer in the bone; he's told her this. But not in her case, he tells me.

Over the phone Mother says she hopes she'll feel better before she gets worse. I suddenly feel as tongue-tied as my father. At last I say, "I hope so too."

She becomes bedridden. Her good right hand trembles, and sometimes doesn't do her bidding; she has to be fed. I drive in to feed her on my visits, my father sometimes accompanying me. But he's a nervous visitor, rising after a few minutes to pace. Then he excuses himself. "I'll be in the parlor," he says to me, referring to the lobby where he waits. When I come to find him he is sitting alone, unoccupied, though all around on tables is a feast of magazines.

Aunt Claire dies. Hospitalized again and again, she finally asked the doctor to let her go. We drive in specially after dark to tell Mother. Despite their mutual affliction, she and Claire had managed to keep up, more recently with phone calls instead of weekly letters.

Mother is silent as she hears the news, but the next morning she says: "I just keep thinking of things to tell her."

I surprise myself by missing Claire too, though I had only seen her in childhood on her summer visits. All my life Claire had lived in the desert of California, fleeing there with a bad husband before my birth. She divorced the husband but stayed in California. With her death I feel that distant desert spot die out. It's as if, glancing up from the yard one day, I discover the uprearing hills of the Missouri River Breaks, south on the horizon, have vanished.

Soon after, Mother announces to me: "You don't have to keep up my diary anymore."

Coarse hairs have sprouted on her chin from the tamoxifen—which isn't working—making her look Chinese-philosopher wise.

I am measuring out pureed plums in a spoon and don't reply.

I finally have the quantity of plums on the spoon just right—too much and it will choke her.

"I've been keeping up your diary so far."

✳

"I wish I'd been more patient with Rosemary," Mother says during one visit.

For a minute I can't speak. My sister has been dead seventeen years, surely long enough to put to rest even her difficult life.

I want to tell Mother the truth, "You were a saint," but I go for something milder.

"You were as patient as anyone could be," I say. I can't believe she would blame herself for Rosemary, whose storms she always countered with mild rebuke.

I chatter to Mother about emotional illness, how aggressive behavior can mask depression—stuff from college. Rosemary was frustrated, I say, brilliant at reading, slow at math. I look down at Mother, who has turned away, her gaze fixed somewhere out the window.

Outside, the sky is trying to turn into spring, raggedy clouds tearing across it

I stop talking; still Mother doesn't turn from where she's staring miles away.

*

On visits I lie in Ginny's former bed each morning—and sometimes in the afternoon—feeling Mother emptying out of my life. I study Ginny's pictures on the walls: a paint-by-number Jesus basking in light; opposite, a hanging on which a bird drawn in liquid embroidery declares in shaky letters, "I'll sing the sweetest song on Mother's Day."

My clothes are crammed inside the closet alongside Ginny's. Boxes on the closet floor hold more of Ginny's clothes, saved through the years by Mother.

My father will have to move into town, I am sure. Someone will have to sort through things. Dad and I don't know how to talk about it. We range around each other, wary, like bygone dogs and cats on our farm.

I know that getting rid of things will be up to me, the family's take-charge person. In a trunk in my parents' old house are Rosemary's things: books and clothing, a road map collection of each state, a handwritten Kennedy family tree.

One day I decide to start with Ginny. I look through clothes on hangers and tumbling off the closet shelf. There are a few things from babyhood: stained shirts, scuffed shoes. Most of the clothes are those in which, to my mother's eyes, she had looked dear. I've seen the '70s flowered bellbottom pants in photos of Ginny with her oriental eyes and big-lipped grin. There is a dark faux fur parka in which she'd squinted toward the camera just before getting fitted for glasses. In boxes on the closet floor are more slacks and tops of polyester knit, worn-out canvas shoes, even socks darned with my mother's patient weave.

When my father is outside, I dump a box into a black trash bag and sneak it to the trunk of my car. The closet still seems full. I fill another trash bag, and another. I swoop clothing off of hangers into bags. I cram eight trash bags into my car's trunk, and pack the last of the clothes—underpants with aged elastic that crumbles at a touch—into a back-seat box.

Once my father walks by as I push a sack into the trunk; he looks away.

I don't know what to do with the cloth wall hanging showing a meadowlark ready to burst into full-throated song. I leave it behind.

At the end of the visit, I creep in the car down my father's rutted road feeling as if I'm carrying Ginny away. I turn west onto the highway toward home, and realize I don't have any idea what to do with Ginny's clothes; they won't fit in my alley can.

Fifty miles away, I reach Wolf Point. I slow through town, then swerve behind a grocery store not yet open for the day. I jump from the car, fling a sack into the dumpster and speed off.

An hour later at Glasgow I leave a bag behind Buttrey Foods—"Go Scotties!" on the marquee—and another one seventy miles farther in wind-swept Malta at the peaceful river park of towering cottonwoods.

On the Fort Belknap Reservation I slip into Horse Capture picnic grounds, tossing a bag into a shiny can.

A hundred miles from Great Falls I drop a bag in Havre at Emporium Food and Fuel—country music blares from a speaker—and another into alley dumpsters along one block. At last I step out of my car to tuck the back-seat box into my own alley's green plastic can.

Then I picture Ginny in pieces, flung out, scattered like stars, across the state.

And I think I know the moment that our family's breakup began. It didn't start at my sisters' deaths, but with their fading in my dying mother's memory. And with the vanishing of their ghostly outlines in all they've owned.

*

In April, Dwight joins me for a visit. The funny weather year continues, bringing skiffs of snow a few days into our stay, though winter should have broken.

Like a miracle, Hazel appears, my brother coaxing her into view. A day later she bounds toward us whenever we step outside.

Our first business is with our dad. Together, we press him to make plans and manage to pin him down: Yes, yes, he says, rising from the table where we've talked. He agrees that sooner or later he'll have to move into town.

Then there's the cat. We've told our mother that Hazel's doing fine. In fact, her snowy fur is lustrous—not from jelly doughnuts—and her eyes are bright. We doubt our father pats her, though. She yowls outside the door, nearly fainting from happiness when Dwight and I appear.

One day he and I settle at the table to make more plans. We've gotten Dad committed to getting the farm appraised, and gained a promise he'll let us help him find a place in town. Now it's time to work on the cat.

"You can't just move a cat," says Dwight, who has two of his own. Dad on the couch ignores us, absorbed in yesterday's newspaper.

"Maybe a neighbor would take her," I say.

My brother frowns, and I think together we imagine her bounding over the miles back to the place she's always haunted.

I look over at Dad, still buried in the newspaper. I decide to startle him into looking up: "Maybe we should shoot her."

But my father doesn't stir. I remember he's shot plenty of things—porcupines, skunks, coyotes, and foxes—and trapped sneaky weasels and mink. When Nip gave birth to pups—thirteen in her doghouse in midwinter—he put twelve in a box, and just outside the yard knocked each on the head with a stick.

"You couldn't shoot a cat," Dwight says. He smiles. "Imagine making Hazel sit still."

We both laugh.

"Leave her here," my brother says. "Let her fend for herself."

Dad suddenly rises and walks outside.

In May when I visit, Mother is restless in bed. "Darn these bedsores," she says.

In the hallway a nurse says to me, "It's bones breaking."

My father and I drive fifty miles to the funeral home in Wolf Point to make some plans. My idea, and it's only after we've arrived that Dad's resistance lowers. As we sit across from the funeral director, he absorbs himself in totaling the costs for burial casket, flowers, thank-you cards, and music.

We arrive back at the hospital barely in time to feed Mother her noon meal. My father, settling down to watch, says in the happy voice that work gives him, "We got some things accomplished today."

Then he stops his story.

For once, Mother doesn't ask him to go on.

When I return alone that evening, my mother won't eat. I offer to snag a nurse in the outside hall for an injection. After I do that, it is time to go, long past when I promised Dad I'd be home for supper. "I hope you feel better," I say automatically. I pause to straighten the slender pile of mail.

My mother has always the same reply: "Oh, I'm bound to." Sometimes: "Don't worry."

Tonight she doesn't answer.

✳

Back in Great Falls, I wait for the call that will bring relief. I know it will be soon.

The call comes in the middle of the night. I know it can be no other; it's 2:00 A.M. I stumble across the darkened living room. Everyone else in the house is asleep.

I hear the nurse begin to talk of Mother. Over the phone, her voice is hushed. I'm reminded that on the other end most everyone is asleep also. Beneath the nurse's soft voice, I can hear the little rushing air of the telephone; I feel as if we two are alone on the face of the earth.

As the nurse calmly tells the account of my mother's death, I have the sensation of becoming completely unanchored, in a way I hadn't known I was anchored before.

∗

A few months later, Dad suddenly sells the farm. Dwight and I meet again on a long weekend to move him to the tiny house he's bought in town. Overwhelmed, we avoid talk of Hazel. She avoids us too; the hustle and bustle of moving frightens her into hiding out.

On our last day, Dwight and I drive out to the farm for odds and ends, and there Hazel waits as always, purring us toward her on the steps. We look around. We are leaving so many things behind already that we stick her into a packing box and head to town. Rain begins, and darkness falls as we arrive. We set the box outside my father's door. We put food and water beside it and slowly open the lid, coaxing Hazel, who is bunched in a corner of the box. Suddenly she leaps, straight upward, and races across the yard, dashing beneath Dad's car.

We pick up the gleam of her eyes in the dark and call to her. She is crouched flat; then a dog barks and she gives a frantic look in its direction. Suddenly, I am aware of a roar of sounds—dogs barking, shouts and laughter from down the street, a car's swish on rainy pavement. Hazel had arrived at my parents' farm at two months of age in midwinter; she spent the first month locked inside the barn. I doubt if ever in her life she has heard dogs or passing cars. When I cross the yard to peer beneath my father's car, she has vanished.

We never see her again.

Daughter

Traveling the narrow highway across the state, my family around me silent, numbed by long miles, I remind myself again that I've survived it: my father selling the farm overnight for a song.

We're headed on a spring visit to someone else's farm, and I've survived that too: Dad selling the farm to no one I cared for, just a young ambitious guy who popped in to visit as Dwight and I unpacked stuff in town. Grinning, he watched us sweat awhile, then zipped away.

In fall my brother and I together survived that change, partly by grasping at little souvenirs as we boxed and moved, a collection of junk from the past to plug the twin holes of the loss of our mother and the farm we'd always known. I asked for Mother's diaries, old postcards, a miniature working sewing machine she'd had as a girl. In the depths of a cupboard, I found the wooden butter paddle: all those years of whirling cream inside the big glass jar churn! We kids spelled each other at the crank till at last butter was formed, then watched Mother press at the clots with the paddle as drops of buttermilk sprang out. In the empty kitchen I lifted the darkened paddle to my face, and inhaled a whiff of rancid butter.

Over the long winter I thought our troubles were smoothing out, but at the beginning of spring another trouble reared.

All my brother had asked for at the move was the John Deere tractor, saved in retirement by Dad. He'd used it to plow Mother's garden and to haul water to their "yard tree," an out-of-element blue spruce that's inched to maybe twenty feet in fifty years of dry prairie life.

I'd learned to drive the John Deere, a simple machine, as a kid. Dwight had a dream of restoring it, toiling year after year in California till at last it ran like new, as none of our dad's marginal machinery had.

So he had asked our father for it in fall. "Okay," Dad said. He seemed surprised. Dwight, after all, had flown the coop right after high school, not saying much to anyone but me: "I'd like to work for someone who thinks I've got brains."

That day my father followed the tractor around as Dwight tried to find a place to store it; the tractor was tall. My brother drove from shed to shed, a farm boy again, maneuvering the tractor expertly from the high seat. He would be back for it in summer, he said, squeezing out from it in the truck garage. Dad popped a tin can over the exhaust to keep out mice, and together they drained the radiator.

Over the winter, my father mentioned the tractor to me on the phone. He'd braved the snowy road to check the farm. "No leaks in the truck garage," he said.

When I called to remind him of my family's spring visit, he remarked casually that the tractor was sold. "He'll be out for it tomorrow," my father said. "A fellow in town who restores them, guess there's money in it."

"Dad!" I said. I don't usually speak up on the phone with him but listen while he vents; I know he's lost without Mother. "That's for Dwight."

There was silence on the other end of the phone. "He's counting on it," I said.

Finally, my father spoke. "Oh, he can't be; he'd never get the thing to California."

I felt desperate. I couldn't picture how a tractor would travel to southern California, but I launched into a lie for my brother.

"He knows someone with a flatbed," I said. I thought that Dwight, always a fixer, probably did know someone like that.

"Dwight really wants that," I pushed, though I knew I was treading dangerously. I'd always been Dad's favorite, something Dwight was nice about. With Mother gone, I was all Dad had. Trying to fill in some of the gaps she left, I talked over old days on the phone, made their kind of jokes. It worked; sometimes at the close of conversation he slipped and called me "wife."

"Ah, heck, he better get a tractor there," my father said. I heard his end of conversation voice.

I called Dwight, who seemed to go into shock over the phone; I tried to hear him breathe. "You've got to call Dad," I said.

On the other end of the phone I felt him hesitate. He's nice like our mother. I told him once that I'm like Dad, short-tempered and always right. He was thoughtful before his reply: "You're not as bad as Dad."

"Call him," I said again.

Instead, my brother described the tractor. "It's a 1947 John Deere A, two-cylinder." I only knew it was John Deere and green. Dwight's voice took on a fond tone others use to talk about their children—he had none.

"It's hard to find a good one; when they set awhile the engine locks. Even on this one I'd change the rings and pistons."

Traveling to visit Mother this year—my brother flying up to me and the two of us driving across the state—he pointed out tractors to me. Even listening with half an ear, I felt soothed by his marking of the farms we passed.

"There's a Steiger Cougar, 250 horsepower."

Passing an orange blur obscured by windbreak, he said, "Huh, an old LA Case."

My brother decided to call Dad. He phoned back to say that our father concurred about not selling the tractor, though Dwight said he was not yet out of the woods. He's always judged Dad harshly, seeing him as lacking sympathy for anyone but himself.

But I've reminded Dwight of times in childhood when another part of Dad emerged. There was our Black Hills vacation. And one Christmas when we were small, we awoke to find a ladder propped against the house, and snowy footprints (a blurry version of our father's overshoes) leading away. On a blizzardy winter afternoon Dad built a rocking horse for Dwight, hand-sawing curved rockers and a box-like seat with neck and head. Then he ventured out into the swirling storm with butcher knife in hand, returning with a ragged fistful of Bud's mane that he tacked onto the wooden neck and seat with fence staples.

Just a day after the tractor crisis seemed settled, I picked up the phone to hear my brother's voice. He'd just talked to a stranger, he said, a man who called him from our father's house. "I don't want to get in the way of family," the man said. "But your father seems to want me to take the tractor."

Dwight said to me over the phone in the disgusted tone he had used when leaving home: "I give up."

✳

It is late afternoon when my family and I reach Culbertson. I slow the car to a crawl as we enter town; despite the all-day drive through soothing hills, my heart still isn't in this. But each year we've visited my folks at the break of spring, this time my father alone. "No more big meals," I remind the kids as we halt in the muddy yard outside the house.

When I first visited Dad in his house alone, I washed the dishes from our canned stew supper and then looked into the refrigerator. A single slice of bread lay on a shelf, and beside it a half jar of store applesauce fantastic with mold. A dark beard of mold spread down toward drinking water in a Mason jar. I found a plump red frankfurter, once the mainstay of our family's diet, alone on a shelf; it made a hollow sound as I bumped it. I took it out and rapped it sharply on the counter's edge; it would not break.

My father pulls open the door at first knock, looking expectant. His broad shoulders fill the doorway of his small house. For years he's seemed the same, just his thick hair whitening. Today he's dressed up in Levis and a western shirt.

Inside, he makes his usual greetings: nodding toward my husband and teenage daughter, then reaching to shake my son's hand. Andy, eleven, is sobered by this; I think no one else shakes his hand.

Dad's single embrace is reserved for me, but when he looks my way I feel myself harden—I can't forget the tractor—and say coolly, "The roads were good." My father blinks. If he is disappointed, he doesn't show it.

We prepare a supper together in the cramped kitchen: bread and butter, canned beef stew, canned peaches, just the basics. I think of the cheerful rattle of my mother crowding dishes onto the table.

It is the next afternoon before we head out to the farm. A few months ago Dad said over the phone that the place was being looted; tools and odds and ends of household stuff whose fate we hadn't determined were being removed.

He mentioned it as an aside, his tone casual, but I felt my guts clench.

My father drives along the highway slowly, all of us packed together in his car. We pass other empty farms edging back to grass, or absorbed into larger holdings. This visit, something else won't be the same. Time will be rolled back: the mobile home is gone, sold to another entrepreneur who has set it up as a rental in town.

What's left is the house I grew up in; we turn off the highway onto the gravel road that leads to the door of the squat white house built chockablock by Dad. I'm surprised again, as I've been each time since returning from college, how small it is.

I'm reminded of a phone call to my brother about the John Deere. Dwight diverted the conversation at the end to his favorite tractor— the powerful Big Bud, Montana-made. He said, "The Bud 500 is taller than our house."

My father pulls into the yard and parks as always just outside the door. Another thing that's upsetting is how easily he refers to the farm as something past. "I went out to the old place," he'll say on the phone. You'd think it had been five years instead of five months since he left it behind!

I stare at the house before stepping out; it's always the same, unfazed by some fifty years of occupation. I don't know the rigors of my father's carpentry, but I have guessed. Once he placed a birdbath in the yard with a heavy one-way disk as the dish, mounting it on a railroad tie dug a foot into the ground. That summer Mother snapped a picture of Dwight and me beside it, the post's wide shadow darkening the grass. For our picture, Dwight and I could have perched on the bath itself.

The house as always gazes at me with its giant eye of kitchen window, but when I step outside the car, something is different. I look around the yard: cow pies everywhere. Dad sees me staring. "The neighbor's cows broke in the first big storm. No one to see it happen."

Mike and the kids scatter to peek in the outbuildings; I follow Dad to the house, walking gingerly. "Don't step on any fresh shoe polish!" he calls back. I look up to see the merriment on his face. I glimpse his other self, what I like to think of as his real self, but today I don't know what to think. His wife is gone, his life's work is in shambles—next year the neighbor's cows may make it into the house itself, rubbing their hides in the doorways my father carefully measured and squared. And he smiles.

But maybe I'm the one who's crazy. I am carrying a camera and extra film, determined to take a picture of every room, perhaps every wall, of the house. And I have brought a newly purchased steel tape to measure the rooms.

I step inside and the first snapshot is easy, the elaborate kitchen cupboard built by Dad. The white paint, chipped from use, still gleams; as a child I imagined the cupboard to be a miniature house itself, the little drawers and shelves its rooms. I poke inside—in jars and in the swingout flour bin are remnants enough of staples from which a last scanty meal could be made.

Next, I take a picture of the washstand, something nice once, perhaps when my father's father owned it before layers of paint clogged the delicate whorls. Always, Dad washed in a basin on it, dripping behind him a darkened trail when he stepped outside to hurl the water out.

I look above the kitchen sink to the tiny cupboard—also built by Dad—where I spy a bottle of his Aqua Velva, always appealing in its foreign ocean blue. Dad shaved before a tiny mirror tacked to the cupboard door. The cupboard is empty except for the bottle, his other shaving things removed. When I squint, I see why this was left; it's the Aqua Velva for ticks, a brainchild of Mother's. Ticks are difficult to kill, flat and hard as seeds; but then my mother thought of aftershave and slipped ticks to an easy, fragrant Aqua Velva death.

I see maybe two dozen ticks in the bottle; I don't take a picture.

I wouldn't have noticed the aftershave at all but the little cupboard doors are opened wide as if—I feel my stomach tighten again—someone has poked and prodded through our house. Did the intruder intend to steal the Aqua Velva, picking it up, then rejecting it upon seeing it was a mausoleum for ticks?

And that's what I mind, I think; not a stranger laughing at us, but the touching and lifting itself. I think of the caution with which Dwight and I occasionally explored the shaving shelf: tickling ourselves with the round badger brush that we carefully balanced on its handle again, daring to touch our fingertips to the long straight razor that we believed dangerous even at rest.

I pass to the tiny living room where a TV set and sagging couch remain—furniture my parents elected not to move next door. Dad crosses to the couch and sinks down; I hear him sigh. In a minute he has retrieved his pocketknife and fiddles with it, snapping the blade. He could have just come in from the fields at noon, recuperating while my mother, noisy at the kitchen cupboard, readies a meal.

Nothing to take a picture of, but then my eye is drawn to the wall opposite the couch. It's the same bland green of my childhood and begrimed, but I remember—and can see by a faint clean square—it is where the piano stood.

Seated beside the dark upright, Dad played his banjo expertly, urging my mother forward through Scandinavian songs: "Styrmans Valsen," the Norwegian river pilot's song, and especially the delicate "Livet i Finnskogarna"—"Life in a Finnish Garden"—that even under my mother's pedestrian fingers managed to sing. Here Mother and I performed duets—"Chatterbox," "Flying Doves"—from her tattery childhood book. We played loud and fast; our triumph was ending a piece together.

I can't photograph the wall. Suddenly, the whole idea of my camera and the tape measure seems foolish. On the couch Dad is silent, drowsing or lost in thoughts of his own. From outside, I hear the shouts of my children making some discovery in a shed.

I think of Dwight and the John Deere tractor—the blank of the garage outside where he had carefully maneuvered it in fall. His desire for the tractor is no crazier than my measuring of empty rooms.

It's the holes in us, I think. My brother imagined a tractor could fill the hole in him, but I think the hole inside him from what Dad did not give is big enough to drive a tractor through.

Always, Dad and Dwight were distant—I remember the glue between my mother and me, pounding out our songs in tandem on the piano.

My father and brother worked together in summer, but Dad liked animals as Dwight didn't, fascinated instead by machinery. According to Dwight, Dad maintained the John Deere badly, skimping on parts.

I step back and seat myself beside my father on the couch; dust rears. The shouts of my family can still be heard outside. Dad, who has not been sleeping, glances at me questioningly.

My mind skips back to an early memory of my brother and father together. Dwight and I had been helping our father—Dwight officially helping him; me standing near. We watched as our father managed on horseback to haze the neighbor's bull into the corral. Then Dad was anxious to phone the neighbor before the agitated bull got an idea about breaking out. "Here," he said, tossing the reins of the horse to Dwight, "tie him to the corral." My brother and I were still small— Bud quibbled with his bit far over our heads. "A half hitch," my father called, already making long strides to the house. Dwight hesitated.

"Can't you tie a half hitch?" My father halted in the dusty path to stare at my brother in disbelief. Even when very young, I hated these moments; I grabbed the reins: "I can."

As Dad continued to the house, I looped the reins securely in a knot he hadn't taught me either, but I'd soaked up how to, hanging at his elbow whenever he saddled the horse. I reached to rub Bud's long black neck, not minding the lather. Then I was surprised to notice my brother's face looking at me from a little distance, furious as the bull's.

When it came time to ride a horse in childhood my brother declined, preferring to travel by bike and red wagon on teeth-jarring roads. I took his place, watching as Dad shortened the stirrups on the worn saddle he'd had since a youth, then finally clambering aboard. I'd studied how Dad handled Bud, and guided him around the yard in a smooth circle as my father beamed.

Now, from beside me on the couch, Dad rises, jiggling his keys. "I'll round everyone up," he says, heading out, though I know there's nothing waiting for him in town.

Outside, where I expect to hear the car revved in impatience, it is silent. I try to imagine the scene: my father pacing the yard hoping the family will get the hint and load up for home. Or just the opposite: deep in conversation with my children. On another visit he led them to the granary where he taught them how to operate the old feed grinder, a relic from his father's time. In the granary is a grindstone, also belonging to my grandfather, a large whirling gray tablet that fascinates my son. Dad turned its crank and promised that one day he'd sharpen my son's knife; I tell Andy he shouldn't count on it.

My erratic father! But he was a loyal companion to Mother: in this living room they'd talk at night as I listened from my darkened bedroom, their low voices propelling me toward sleep.

I've been feeling a little peeved that, with Mother gone, Dad hasn't slipped on a little of the mantle she cast off: inquiring about the kids' activities at school, laying in a supply of food for our visit. But I think that Mother's absence won't alter Dad's continued absorption in the one who rescued him from isolated cabin life. On quiet evenings he sat in the kitchen watching her at chores.

Did Dad find such comfort in my mother's presence because the only other woman in his life—the mother who fled home to teach in rural schools—scarcely comforted him at all?

I am startled by voices close outside the house. For a minute I can't think whose they might be. My God, I've become my father: lost in convolutions of thought as life goes on!

I step outside and see at the far edge of the yard the only family I have left, except for my brother. They stand in motley formation, my children shoulder-to-shoulder, a little shrunk from my father, who gesturingly speaks. My husband, too, stands at a little remove from Dad, though leaned politely forward to listen. What's missing, of course, is Mother, who would have bound us together with her smile and fluttering worry over the visit.

Suddenly, I see at my son's side a newly sharpened knife, and in front of him the yard tree—cut down.

I walk over as fast as I can. "What happened?" I ask Dad. Of course,

Andy didn't do it. But the tree has been cut, I see, from the trunk's clean edge.

"Oh, they had to cut it down to pull the trailer out," my father replies. At least he doesn't joke.

The tree looks like a fallen giant on its side. In its infancy it was once Rosemary's height. In a glossy gray photo in our mother's album, she stands shoulder-to-shoulder with the tree, her smile broad.

Now, as if the tree itself can't quite believe it, some of the branches, tucked against the trunk, look fresh, though the mobile home was hauled away months ago.

Everyone stares at the tree. Still carved around the stump is the circular ditch that my father in summer would fill with water hauled behind the John Deere. I'd done it a time or two myself: pulling the barrel on skids to the weedy dam where bucket-by-bucket I filled it to the brim, enjoying getting soaked under the heat. Then I turned the tractor around to drive home slowly as big drinks of water slopped out onto prairie grass.

Finally, I say, "You hauled a lot of water to that tree."

I expect my father to brush me off or form a joke; instead he looks straight at me:

"Yes, I did."

*

My father drives home slowly, and back at his house in town is another surprise. I discover it accidentally, following him into the garage to locate a broom (I don't think he's swept out his place since my last visit). On the floor of the garage is—I can't think of anything else—my mother's coffin. The rich brown surface gleams even under dim light.

But it's not a coffin at all, I see when my senses return, but her large cedar chest.

She obtained her hope chest as a teenager. The veneer is still smooth, acquiring only a handful of scratches in its long life. At my father's move, my brother and I carried it perilously down the steep pitch of stairs to the basement. I try to picture Dad pulling it up again.

My father returns from a corner of the garage with his excuse for a broom, its edges curled like the fluffy bangs I yearned for as a child. I point to the chest: "What are you doing with that?"

"Oh, I'm going to varnish it, get rid of it. It takes up space down there."

I take a breath. "You can't get rid of Mother's cedar chest!"

Of course, I knew I would own the chest some day, though I wasn't in a hurry. Inside was treasure that we kids were occasionally allowed to finger through: valentines from Mother's youth with their crabbed signatures; her piccolo, accompanied by a photo in which she holds it smartly in the school band, a sheaf of greeting cards congratulating her on marriage; a ribbon-tied box of our baby clothes whose names we liked to repeat—"kimono," "soaker."

I release the catch and lift the chest's lid. Then I can barely contain a panic: "Where's all her stuff?"

"Oh, there wasn't much of anything," Dad says. He strolls away to the darkest corner of the garage. "It's here and there around the basement," he calls back.

I was irritated when Dwight gave up on the tractor too soon, but now I feel defeated myself and turn away: If he doesn't want me to have the chest, forget it.

I fix supper for us my father's style, opening cans of things. My kids pick at the pork and beans, Vienna sausages, and creamed corn, appalled. Dad doesn't seem to notice—does he notice anything? I've been deliberately cool toward him since discovering the chest in the garage. I'm formulating a plan of survival, cutting myself loose from him—what Dwight did when he left home years ago. I'll pretend I'm not his daughter. It's what he calls me over the phone—"daughter"—when he doesn't slip and call me "wife."

Well, I won't be. I feel it as a divorce. No more comforting calls on the phone; just an occasional letter, polite. In my suitcase I've packed an extra phone from my house, and the wire and tools to extend it from the kitchen wall to his bedside; I'd planned the chore with Mike following our meal. No more. While washing the dishes, rattling them in their pan at the sink, I picture my father waking one morning gripped by heart attack or stroke. No phone to call for help, no one to check on him. He'll die alone, neglected, as he's turned his back on my brother and me: our revenge.

That evening when Dad's gone to bed—8:30 on the dot—my

husband tries to comfort me with words he's said before. His field is mental health. "Remember your father's background," he says. "It's hard to give what you haven't yourself been given."

I know the stories, mostly told by Mother. Beginning at age nine, Dad stayed home alone during his father's overnight grain-hauling trips, commanded to feed the livestock and cook his own meals too. The homestead shack was far from neighbors; the prairie at night was black. Dad slept with a gun.

My father, in turn, failed Dwight; he did not try to lead or persuade. He did not lure Dwight into farming but simply announced at supper one night that twelve-year-old Dwight was old enough to help with harvest. Dwight learned to drive the pickup, edging it in stubble fields alongside the engorged combine to receive its load. He learned to start the engine on the auger that whirled wheat up to the roof opening of the steel bin. He ignored the engine's jolt of electric shock at its start, just as the men did. Each evening he came home tired, and ate his late supper in silence as if he were grown.

My father took parenting instructions from his father's playbook. "The children shirk everything they can," Grandfather lamented when his son and daughter were still small. At Christmastime one year, with his family united on the homestead, he wrote of Bill and Mary, nine and eleven years old: "The children do not want to sing. I have to drive them to it."

I know my father's sufferings. I pity him. But it's time for me to make a clean break.

The next morning my family leaves as scheduled. The abbreviated visit was planned; in the tiny house my kids had to sleep on the living room floor's linoleum.

Dad fixes for breakfast again a huge amount of cooked cereal, apparently refusing to believe that my children turn up their noses at it. The kids pour into their bowls stale Cheerios—bought by Mother on a previous visit—while I try to eat a share of their Cream of Wheat.

I look at their blond heads bowed over cereal and think how spoiled they are.

I wonder how they'll treat me when I'm old.

Then Dell, as if gaining courage from stirring her cereal, looks up to ask Dad: "Can I have the cedar chest?"

My father looks startled, then his face begins to light. His clear blue eyes—his best feature and one that I have inherited—gleam. "Why, sure!" he says.

After breakfast, while we pack the car, he measures the cedar chest and decides a single sheet of plywood will make a crate. He's excited, as if he thought of the idea himself. He decides what tools to use and calculates the project will take one day. I picture the sturdy crate he'll build that may outlast the cedar chest itself. I'll call a freight company at our arrival home, the one traveling across the state from North Dakota.

I ride away in the car in wonder: at my teenage daughter so often sunk in self-absorption who confides she has done this for me, at my father who has somehow been roused to the role of grandfather to her.

On the trip home I feel myself turn back to him, somewhat against my will. My yielding reminds me of a theory about the failure of dieting: the body has a "set point" in weight toward which it always struggles to return when pounds are shed.

Then things don't go smoothly with the chest. The next day when I phone Dad he balks. The price of plywood has gone up (I've said I'll pay the bill).

"Couldn't you find a chest cheaper there?"

I call the trucking company. The woman allows as how a crate wouldn't have to be built, just the surface of the chest needing protection. Feed sacks or a strip of insulation would do. I call Dad back, pushing him; he seems a little peeved. Impatient, he says he'll find some feed sacks left behind on the farm.

My mercurial father! His enthusiasm for shipping the chest has vanished. I spend the next day unpacking things, including the extension phone which goes back onto a shelf, and wonder if the chest will arrive at my door.

I yearn for the chest, though I can't think what to put inside it and don't even know where it can fit in our house.

I'm reminded of a Big Bud story of Dwight's. He was traveling on a visit home, not hurrying; soon enough he would feel again the gulf caused by his leaving—our parents were always silent toward his California life. He was taking the time to cruise through tractor dealerships fringing small towns. Suddenly, he glimpsed a machine he'd only seen in pictures: a 500-horsepower Bud, the silver giant taller than our house.

He slowed the car and stopped. He got out, and found himself mounting a ladder to the railed deck, then trying the cab door. To his surprise it was unlocked; he stepped inside.

"It was like a big beautiful room," he said.

He wasn't interested in examining the buttons and knobs, the two-way radio and tape deck, not even the electronic screen displaying tire slippage. He sat down inside the cab.

He kept waiting for someone to shoo him out. He saw faces staring at him from the dealer's window, but no one came.

"I just sat there the longest time," Dwight said. "I don't know why."

Now as I wait for the cedar chest to arrive, I feel Dwight's longing. I scour my memory for times I thought Dad loved me, an antidote to the acid hurt of his wanting to sell the chest as if it were one more object instead of soaked in family history. What is so broken inside him that he can't see Mother in the pretty chest, and hope to pass a particle of that to me?

I latch onto a remembrance of my parents' single visit to Great Falls. I plucked them from the train in Havre, and two hours later turned into my leafy one-way street. As we drew up to the house, an old one in need of remodeling but twice the size of our farm home, Dad breathed: "This is how I always hoped your life would be."

Mostly, I recall referred love from visits home when the kids were small. If there's referred pain—felt beyond an injury site—why not referred love?

From his couch perch, Dad studied my energetic children at play. When Andy solved a small problem with Tinkertoys my father declared, "Your son shows ingenuity." I felt myself warm. Once when my daughter came in empty-handed from the nestboxes, Dad rose and crossed to the refrigerator. He slipped two eggs from the shelf into deep pockets of his overalls. A few hours later Dell bore the eggs inside in triumph after a chicken house visit.

A week passes; no chest arrives. Then it suddenly appears outside my door. But it doesn't look like itself at all with a green blanket around it, one I remember from childhood. The blanket is not tied on; my father has unbraided a length of rope and woven its skeins through slits cut carefully along the blanket's edge. As if sewn on, snug and protective except for a gap, several inches wide, across the top where the blanket ends don't meet.

Something he just didn't see?

But I'm so glad to have Mother's cedar chest; I hug it at the door. I discover a wooden hinge is broken; it's had some banging around.

I can fix the wooden hinge with clamps and glue. What I can't fix, and I see every time I look at the chest, is a scratch it suffered from the blanket's gap. It's a deep scratch, odd-shaped, reminding me of Chinese characters or hieroglyphics. Something—like the years of my childhood, and the years with my father remaining—I can't translate.

Afterword: Ghost

2003

For two years after the house was burned, I didn't return home; now I've set out on a quest. I want to discover the cause of death of Paul Bisceglia. He didn't die yesterday or even in my childhood, but ninety years ago. Why do I care? His house was a ghost house, the empty homestead cabin between our farm and that of our grandparents, perched on a hill above the highway. Dwight and I hiked to it in summers, stepping inside to view a sturdy child's chair, a cozy corner shelf still faintly blue, a tiny shoe stiff as iron with age. Dad farmed the land, still owned by Bisceglias in far-off Chicago, and planted wheat up to the door. The shack was sturdy—built of bridge timbers Paul Bisceglia had been lucky enough to acquire. It had two dark eyes of windows, and a door stuck ajar. I pictured Louisa Bisceglia failing to close it as she rushed back to Chicago with three small children after finding Paul's body hanging.

He couldn't make a living from the land. Perhaps he killed himself because he was lonely, an Italian cast among Scandinavians. Or his wife was fooling around with the priest (Grandpa Hawkins's version; he had learned to hate the Pope in his Swedish childhood). Or maybe he suffered depression, another Paul Bisceglia says over the phone. "Maybe he needed medication."

I found this Paul in the Chicago phone book. Yes, he was named after *the* Paul Bisceglia, as was his father. The original Paul Bisceglia was a great uncle, his grandfather's brother. This Paul is cheerful. If melancholy undid his uncle, the malady has skipped generations or died out. The nephew is sure that Paul worked on the railroad in Montana before homesteading. He thinks Paul shot, rather than hanged, himself.

On a clear fall day I set out for home, drawn along the narrow highway north and then east paralleling the Missouri River. Three hundred forty miles away, and fifty miles short of home, I stop outside the Roosevelt County Courthouse in Wolf Point. It's another dying small Montana town. I'm shocked to see the Wolf Point Saddlery boarded up after all these years. I liked to walk its aisles as a kid to inhale the smell of leather.

Inside the compact stucco courthouse, signs point upstairs to the Clerk and Recorder, and down to the county's misery in the basement: Welfare Department, County Nurse, Alcohol and Drug, Mental Health. Upstairs at the end of a quiet hallway, the clerk and recorder sends me packing: this has been a county only since 1919, when it split from Sheridan County a hundred miles away.

I head east again, passing a small church just off the highway outside Wolf Point. On my last visit home I drove up to the high-steepled building, identified on its sign as an Indian Presbyterian Church. More than half of our county is Fort Peck Reservation land. The church was clearly abandoned, white paint peeling, but the adjoining prairie graveyard wasn't. I saw old graves and new graves, most marked by homemade wood or concrete crosses. The grave of a young woman, twenty-eight, glittered with coins and a sealed can of beer. The newest member of the cemetery, Arthur Bigleggins, fifty-six, had a bottle of water, a travel coffee mug (half full), and a pack of Parliaments to send him on his way. I feel a tug toward the cemetery as I pass by, but I'm in a hurry to reach Sheridan County.

A half hour later, I do stop at the cemetery before Culbertson, though it will delay my trip to Plentywood fifty miles north. My parents are buried near the graves of my sisters and Dell Hawkins, on a rise of hill overlooking fields and pasture.

When I stopped here last time, I felt myself in the presence of my parents, or as close to them as I could come. I told my mother, speaking to her gravestone, that I was sorry she had died, but from my father I wanted answers. I know he was lost without Mother, but why did he choose her headstone without consulting my brother and me? On the prairie all around are tombstones short and tall, elaborate and plain; one family is cozy inside a picket fence. Some stones announce MOTHER and FATHER, or MOM and DAD. Visiting after my mother's death, I found a red granite marker with a rose and WIFE engraved.

"Wife?" my brother repeated over the phone. "Did we not exist?"

I also asked Dad why he couldn't seem to love his son. I can't recall Dad giving Dwight a compliment or proud gaze. When Dwight went into the Marines, and then to California, leaving the farm behind, our father seemed to forget him. Once he asked me during a visit home if Dwight lived in California or Nevada.

A few days after Dad's death in 2000, Dwight and I stood together in a quiet viewing room staring into our father's casket. I experienced déjà vu: forty-three years before, I had stood beside the casket of my father's father, also aged ninety. I looked over at Dwight. In California he had graduated from junk cars to Lincolns, driving one seventeen hundred miles in two days for the funeral. I asked: "Do you feel any better about him now that he's gone?"

"No," Dwight said.

I'm still astonished at the easy affection between my husband and son—mock headlocks, jokes, and teasing. Their banter soothes me but also painfully reminds me that Dad's relationship with Dwight was hollow.

This visit to the cemetery, I kneel beside my mother's grave and tell her I still miss her. I stare at my father's stone. To match our mother, my brother and I arranged for a red granite marker on which stalks of wheat and HUSBAND are carved, finalizing our nonexistence.

Of course, we could have made Dad's marker as we pleased, and changed Mother's too. Dwight could have pushed Dad harder for the John Deere tractor. But we yearn for something more. What shines from the dark varnished surface of my mother's cedar chest—a little forlorn in its corner of our basement—is the memory of Dell wanting it for me.

I get back into the car, and at Culbertson turn north onto the road that travels straight to Plentywood just below the Canadian line. I discover at my arrival that the cemetery stop has made me late; the Sheridan County Courthouse is closed. I find the only motel in town, the Sherwood Inn: *Welcome Hunters! Welcome Canadians!* The entrance admonishes *Wipe Your Feet*, and a sign above my room's sink cautions against using towels for cleaning boots or game.

I sit beneath a window overlooking the quiet street, and dial Great Falls. My husband sounds lonely over the phone. We're empty nesters now. I wonder as we talk why I've made so many trips here, leaving my family behind. Perhaps I can't break away because the memories are so hard to shrug off.

All these years later, I can't shrug off feeling poor. I rinse out plastic bags and prefer to dry clothes on a basement rack. Mike has become resigned to how his gifts of new garments hang in my closet a year or more before I'll wear them: I like to peek inside to view a blouse with tags dangling—new clothes!

The list goes on, as if poverty is encoded in my DNA. From a college class I loved I can't recall a single poem—just that the poet Cesar Vallejo was so poor that he trained himself to walk and sit in ways that would preserve his shoes and trousers. Our young children were treated to an extravagant vacation (Disneyland, Mike's idea), during which they rarely ate out (cereal and sandwich fixings brought along at my insistence). I routinely let magazine subscriptions lapse, then start them up again at an introductory rate—this on a middle-class income in Great Falls.

Effects of the homesteading adventure linger in a fourth generation. Dell in Bozeman buys good clothes, skis, a mountain bike, but complains over the phone that she feels guilty after every purchase. Andy, who reversed the family migration to propel himself east to school, has lived so austerely on his scholarship that he may graduate with money in the bank.

Early the next morning, I walk back along the highway toward downtown, then east to the courthouse on Main Street. Plentywood is a pretty town, surrounded by deep coulees and high bluffs, distinct from the rolling prairie all around. It lies on the Missouri Couteau, angling down from Canada and on through the Dakotas, a once-stationary edge of the retreating and advancing Wisconsin glacier. In the glacier's several-thousand-year pause here, it dropped a mess of till forming steep ridges, and blocks of ice whose eventual melting pocked the countryside with small sloughs. This was headquarters for Dutch Henry, whom Grandpa Hawkins and other early homesteaders feared. His gang stole horses and hid them in brush-lined coulees and breaks. Now the area is a headquarters for deer, drawing hunters.

On the second floor of the courthouse, I hand the clerk a three-by-five card on which I've printed PAUL BISCEGLIA. She disappears and I hold my breath. But I strike out. "Of course we've only been a county since 1913," the clerk says, "when we were split from Valley County." She assures me that the Valley County seat 150 miles away in Glasgow, which I drove through on my trip to Wolf Point, is the one I seek.

I get into my car to backtrack south and west, but at Culbertson I detour east from town. The familiar road stretches ahead; in ten miles I'll meet but two cars, no one I know. I pass classmates' farm homes now occupied by nonfarmers, or by part-time ones who also work in town. Many stand empty—like the shingled cottage on the Nelson place—and as the last of the homestead shacks crumble, become this century's relics.

On another visit here I saw that the fence between Nelson's place and my grandparents' had been pulled down. The farms appeared closer; it seemed a glimpse back in time to early homestead years. I stopped the car and crossed the prairie to find where the fence had been. Only with effort could I locate slight posthole scars. What had seemed so dominating in my youth—taut fences that declared *your land, my land*—were mere pinpricks on the prairie mat, easily healed.

Removing fences is part of large-scale farming, the latest experiment on the northern plains. No doubt its adherents believe it is the land's destiny. The number of farms in Roosevelt County has been reduced by half in thirty years, though the total acreage is nearly the same. Our family's 450-acre farm, half of it cropland, was good-sized in my childhood, an area my dad could seed, weed, and harvest with his wide-front 60-horsepower Case tractor. Now 2,000 acres is the county average, and 300-horsepower tractors are routine.

History does not haunt here. Wind has its way with old homesteads, tugging them down, absolving those who've failed, and leaving no monuments to warn newcomers.

At last I turn off the highway and cross the cattle guard to creep up our grassy road. All of our farm roads—north to the tree-fringed dam, west toward the Bisceglia house over the horizon—are grown over. The new owner has placed more land into the Conservation Reserve Program. He collects government money, as each year the farm remembers more of what it was before the introduction of roads and wheat.

I glance at the remains of house settling deeper into burned decay. Nature is earnestly trying to seam over our occupation here with fierce stands of fireweed on ground fouled by ashes and junk. Tall plants woven through the metal bedstead sway in the wind. A lone stalk waves merrily from a stovepipe-cum-flowerpot, devout in its belief of permanence, though a series of grasses will nudge it out.

I turn and head downhill to the long red barn, wading through waist-high brome grass: what a year! Rain when the country needed it; I can't remember bottom grass this tall in my childhood. I pull open the chicken house door on the barn's west end and see in dim light the gleam of three pole roosts, bleacher-style, polished by years of chicken feet. Opposite are five nestboxes. I'm not on the hunt for souvenirs, but I find one on the floor below: a white ceramic insulator, my mother's cheap nest egg for the orange crate boxes. It has a chicken manure streak; I think of the fever to hunt dinosaurs in our state, including their manure: "coprolite." I slip the insulator knob into my pocket. My parents sold their small flock fifteen years ago. When does manure change to something else?

I leave the chicken house and walk past windbreak trees, now in gaunt-limbed death. At the granary, I roll open the door with its little growl. I see a litter of objects I've rejected as souvenirs: tin cans of bolts and screws; Goldy's rope halter, greasy from use; a mayonnaise jar with a dark substance that has reverted to something elemental. But on the floor is something new: a thick book with a maroon cover.

The only books in our granary were on the rafters above, where my father kept his father's diaries in an ancient camelback trunk, and his books in two boxes that mice liked to chew through. This must be newly fallen from the rafters. I squint to read the title: *An Outline of World History in Four Volumes: Part I.*

The book is Grandfather Alexander's, of course. I see not just a history of the world—part one—but a history of my father's family. My grandfather was a dreamer, a poor parent and provider. Dad would launch into riffs about things his "educated fool" of a father had done: Lost in thought as he re-roofed the chicken house one spring day, he overlapped shingles the wrong way. In a drought year when root vegetables were needed for the winter cellar, he put half the garden into watermelon, hoping to boil the juice into sugar. "Had our first taste of ranch watermelon," he recorded: "Fine as silk."

My father hated how his father pored over agriculture yearbooks, histories, and his diaries, resorting to a magnifying glass as he aged—but Dad saved them all!

Now my grandfather's diaries have vanished. In 1995 news spread fast of Dad's abrupt farm sale. Tools began to disappear, and when I arrived and rolled open the granary door, the trunk was gone. I picture it as a curiosity in someone's house in town, a third- or fourth-generation Montanan separated from the family farm by this decade's drought. The inked pages—about 1,798,720 words, I once calculated—perhaps reside in the Culbertson dump. Or strewn along a prairie coulee: pages turning brittle under summer sun, a million words dissolving in snow.

I stare at the handsome maroon book resting on a sift of mouse droppings and bright pink-treated seed wheat, and remember my foolish grandfather and the sufferings he caused his son. Perhaps it's time to forgive my father, or at least to shed the arrogant belief that he purposely withheld interest in Dwight and me.

My mind flashes back to a visit with Dad to the empty farm. We rambled along dirt paths between the sheds and barn, then Dad stood silent in the prairie yard, looking around at all that had gone out of his life. Growing up, I observed that the wind-delivered scent of grass was sweeter in spring than in fall; in summer I felt inside me the fierce sun ripening our wheat. But now I think I can't begin to understand the depth of my father's intimacy with this land, his trigger of memory for each bit of scarred ground, fences and roads, and the jumble of discarded machinery near the windbreak. And I can't begin to apprehend his level of disappointment in Dwight for leaving this behind.

Almost certainly, Dad's devotion to his land played a part in Dwight's drifting away. Dad preferred the outdoors—observing crops and cattle, sensing shifts in wind and weather—to the tangle of family life inside the house.

I get into the car and at the highway turn back toward town. Past town I slow at the cemetery, but remind myself I'm on the way to Glasgow. I whiz through quiet country, fields harvested, grass cured on hills. Everything is silent, waiting for the force of winter. I meet few cars. In fall my parents were subdued, quiet in the kitchen when we kids burst in off the lumbering bus from school.

I reach Glasgow with time to spare, and though the town is bigger and busier than any other in my round-the-state courthouse tour, I find the building right away on Main Street and park in front. Inside, I place my index card on the counter, but the clerk at her desk doesn't rise. She motions me, and I slip through a door, following her to a corner of the office with a tall shelf. "You can look through the book yourself," she says. Then she draws from the shelf an unwieldy volume whose title makes my heart leap: *Register of Deaths I.*

I've forgotten why I want to know it, but buried in these pages is the real cause of Paul Bisceglia's death.

I place the cream-colored book on a table that the clerk has cleared, and open to page one.

Inked in a spidery hand is the first entry: *J.C. Brown, alias Pigeon-toed Kid. Age: approx. 25 years. Occupation: Horseman. Born: Danforth, Illinois. Cause of Death: Bullet wound. April 29, 1908.*

I scan down; on just one page the causes of death are *tubercular, bronchial pneumonia, bowell trouble, suicide, drowning, accidental drowning, dysentery.* Mary T. Wizzen, six months, died of *summer complaint.* Alva Howard Hardenburg, six years, five months, was *shot by 22 rifle accidentally.*

I take a breath. This, I think, is an outline of the history of the world.

I discover that no one, except for small children, was born here; everyone died far from home. Alva Howard Hardenburg's mother and father were from Iowa and New York; they grieved without family. Though John Kawalski, thirty-five, from Russia, was single, an *informant* reported his death in patient detail: *Thrown by horse and was dragged by rope attached to a bronc which he was leading.*

Six pages later, it dawns on me that I'm now reading of deaths in 1920. Paul Bisceglia couldn't have died later than 1912. I scan the reports, and notice that none are of deaths farther east than Poplar, sixty miles away; Culbertson was forty miles farther on a dirt track. There's not a single Culbertson death.

I ask two busy clerks where the death might be recorded. They don't know. A third clerk has been planning dinner over the phone—"how about hamburgers on the grill?"; she swivels in her seat to stare.

I close the book and slip out of the room to retrace my journey home. Paul Bisceglia will remain a ghost. My parents will stay mum in their underground caves in the cemetery.

But something has changed. Somewhere between the maroon book fallen from the rafters, and the acute details of *Register of Deaths I*, the sting of my father's indifference lessened.

Driving home I feel the presence of Arthur Bigleggins and the new Paul Bisceglia. We're all about the same age, a year or two apart, well into our middle years. Arthur Bigleggins has been the least fortunate of us, his journey cut short. His forebears, the original eastern Montana inhabitants, had their land stolen, and their way of life—roaming after bison—destroyed. The 1874 treaty ceding to natives one-fifth of our state was rolled back twelve years later to a fraction of its size. Perhaps Bigleggins's grandfather was among those my grandfather occasionally observed on the Indian trail from Fort Union to Fort Benton a mile south of his land. Grandpa Hawkins would not have been cruel toward the hungry, displaced natives, but he was comfortable with the idea of whites succeeding them, at ease with the mores of his day. On July 13, 1904, in his record of itinerant jobs he worked during his first Montana year, he wrote: "Been cowpunching all day and helped to round up the cattle for the night, got a situation from Baker. Dug up an Indian grave but found nothing."

Paul Bisceglia from Chicago told me that his ancestors' Montana venture is only the dimmest of family memories, though he surprised me—and maybe himself—by remembering Bainville, the small town now almost a ghost town where his great uncle first worked. This Paul has left behind his family's ethnic neighborhood and moved to the suburbs. He does not seek out other Italians, though he accompanies his brother to meetings of an association of Italian lawyers.

Why would Paul Bisceglia remember Bainville? What determines our ties? When at last my Hawkins grandparents left the homestead—moved by Claire to California when Grandma's eyesight dimmed—my grandfather cheerfully put sixty-five years in Montana behind. "This is frosting on the cake!" he wrote from the mobile home's spare room. Under the staggering desert heat, he managed to grow two vines of plump Concord grapes.

Grandma missed trinkets that she'd liked to examine in her dresser drawer. She worried that skunks would move beneath the barn and sheds. She wrote in her diary: "No wind." "Still no wind." "No wind here." Two years later and a month before her death—followed by burial in a desert cemetery—I received a last letter from her. In large, loopy scrawl she wrote: "Last night I dreamed I crawled back home."

At the end of my trip, as after every visit home, I call Dwight. I ask him again, "Do you still wish you hadn't grown up there?"

This time he surprises me. "No," he says, "I'm glad." He pauses. "I guess I've lost the hostility of youth."

Then he's not sure just what he's plucked of value from our past. "I guess it gave me the determination to never be poor again," he says. "I knew when I moved to California I would not get into drugs and lose my way. I'd make money."

"And has that made you happy?" I wonder.

"Yes."

He goes on to say that he still hates some of what he endured on the farm. He particularly disliked shoveling wheat augured from above into the round bin, a chore he performed at age twelve, "when I became a hired man." Hour after hour as the temperature soared inside the bin, he pushed wheat around. At night he tried to sleep with prickles of dust and chaff on his skin—baths were still rationed in summer. "The next day I got up and pulled on dirty clothes and did it all over again."

I'm glad I grew up on the farm, though I hate how that life beat my grandparents and parents down, and circumscribed the lives of my brother and me. Dwight is bright but didn't get a college education. After getting my degree, I called myself a writer for two decades but lacked the confidence to start a book. Only in 1994, as I watched my life in eastern Montana slip away, did I conquer the fear to begin a long-considered family tale. On the drive home after visiting my ill mother in Culbertson, I pulled into a farm approach and scribbled the first words under the watchful gaze of a herd of Angus cattle.

I've hoped through writing this to get clues into my grandparents. Would they have wished to reverse the grinding wheel of history that delivered them to far-flung Montana?

My Grandmother Alexander, the schoolteacher, smiling as she smoothed her clean apron on our visits to her in town, would have said *yes*.

It's hard to imagine Grandfather Alexander, clinging stubbornly to his hopeless homestead until nearly forcibly removed by his wife and son, preferring to live somewhere else. The afflictions of his farm mirrored the turmoil inside his head.

Grandpa Hawkins, brimming with enthusiasm for crazy schemes—encapsulating hydrochloric acid, bombing foxes, turning arid prairie into farmland—would stay. He was the poster boy for homesteading, relishing the work of throwing up sheds and barns and fences with his two hands. He was in part lured west by James J. Hill, who distributed pamphlets to entice settlers along his recently completed Great Northern Railway:

> North Dakota, the Sunshine State: an Abundance of Summer Sunshine, Cool Nights in Warm Season and Bracing Cold in Winter Makes This State an Ideal Dwelling Place.

My grandfather was caught in a blizzard during his first "bracing" Montana winter. He struggled toward home, finally sitting on a rock to rest. He passed out and woke up almost frozen stiff, at last managing to fall off the rock and wallow in the snow till he could move his limbs again and stumble home.

Did Grandma Hawkins wish that she had raised her family in safe and settled Minnesota instead? Her sisters there did not lose children. Never mind, she bloomed where she was planted. Anyone who can observe in her diary "20 below but calm and so nice out" has made peace with her country. I still dream of walking with her through the corral, dried manure crumbling beneath our feet, into open prairie.

I return on trips and in my dreams to a lonely corner of Montana because it is a source. It's an origin of my tendency toward isolation that Mike mourns, but I am also entangled with the hope of this place, even now busily renewing itself following the ravages of early twentieth-century farming.

Just recently, there was another change: the new owner swapped farming for carpentry instead. He turned over the farm to his brother-in-law, an even larger landowner, and now drives each day to Sidney to work on a vast enlargement of the town's hospital and nursing home. He's part of our area's expanding industry of caring for a graying population. My classmates and I left behind our aging parents, the sons and daughters of homesteaders, as we fled.

In college I learned that grass is the "climactic species" of this land. It was nature's design for grass to beat everything else out. Even wheat, and therefore, my family.

I come back home to feel myself in the presence of my family—so deeply, briefly here, and to witness the triumph of the grass.

Acknowledgments

First thanks go to Dwight, always good-humored toward my need to stir up the past.

Thanks to Janet Henderson, Irene Wanner, and Pete Fromm for their critiques, and to Mary Clearman Blew and Judy Blunt for encouragement when I needed it.

My thanks to Sheila Saxby for her love and support, for her insight about our shared Alexander grandparents, and for permission to quote from her mother's unpublished compilation of Grandfather's diaries, which clear-eyed Aunt Mary titled "An Enterprise of Doubtful Value."

I am grateful to the Montana Arts Council for the fellowship that funded my travels. I am indebted to Melba Pattillo Beals's book *Warriors Don't Cry* (Simon & Schuster, 1994) for details about the Little Rock Nine.

Special thanks to Chuck Rankin at the University of Oklahoma Press who envisioned a book from disjointed essays, and patiently prodded me toward it. Thanks also to copy editor Jay Fultz for his hard work that added much clarity to the book.

Finally, a nod to my forebears—William and Mary Alexander, Charlie and Ella Hawkins, and Bill and Norma Alexander—without whom this work would not exist. Ardent diarists, letter writers, and storytellers, they provided much material, and also modeled for me that language and history matter.

＊

Earlier versions of five chapters of this book have been previously published as follows:

"Violets" in *Under the Sun* 3 (Summer 1998)
"Daughter" in *The New Orphic Review* 2 (Fall 1999)
"Journey" in *North Dakota Quarterly* 67 (Winter 2000)
"Haircut" in *The Cream City Review* 24 (Fall 2000); and in *The New Montana Story: An Anthology*, edited by Rick Newby (Helena, Mont.: Riverbend Publishing, 2003)
"Destiny" in *Montana Women Writers: A Geography of the Heart*, edited by Caroline Patterson (Helena, Mont.: Farcountry Press, 2006)